Creative Nature Coloring Book:

Secret Magic in the Forest

Ariel Paglia

All pictures are **Copyright Free images** mainly taken from author's private collection. It's sole purpose is relaxation and stress free painting.

This book is just a paperback of these images –compiled with the best hope – to serve you and to help people all around the world to relax and enjoy in coloring books.

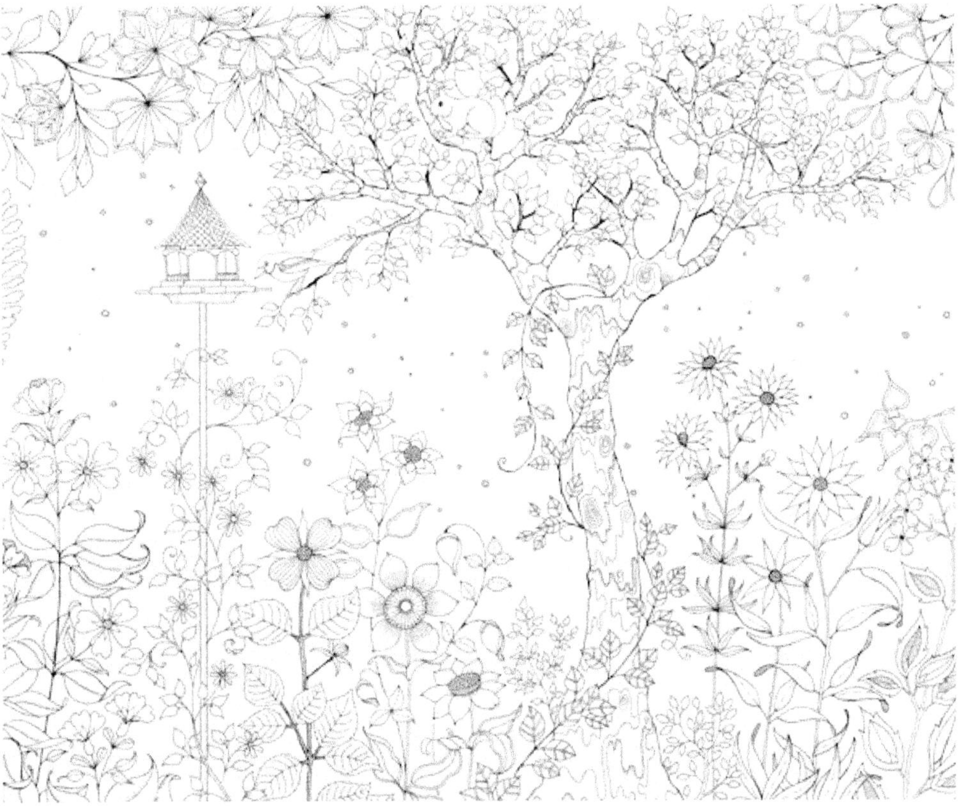

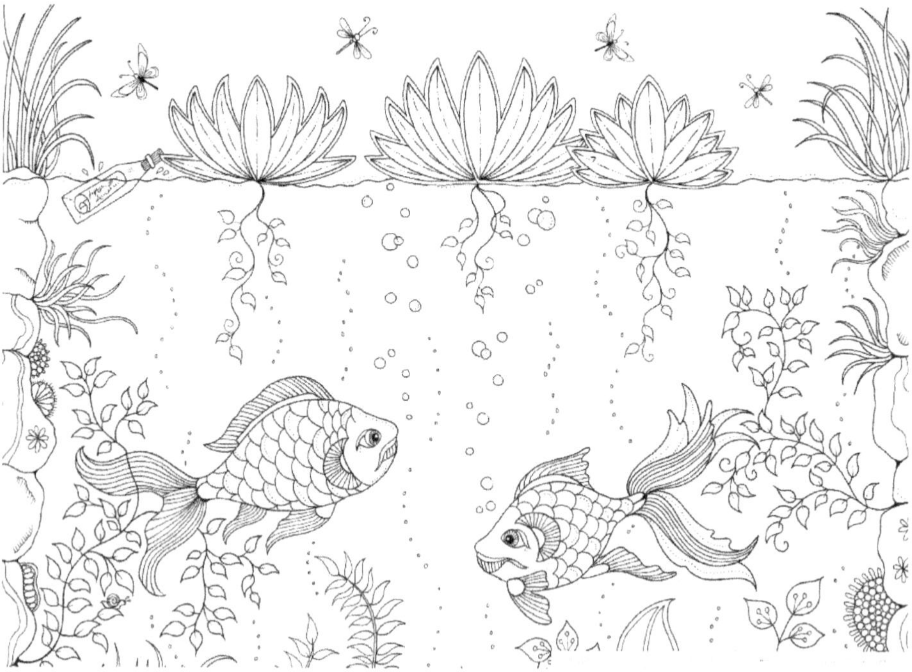

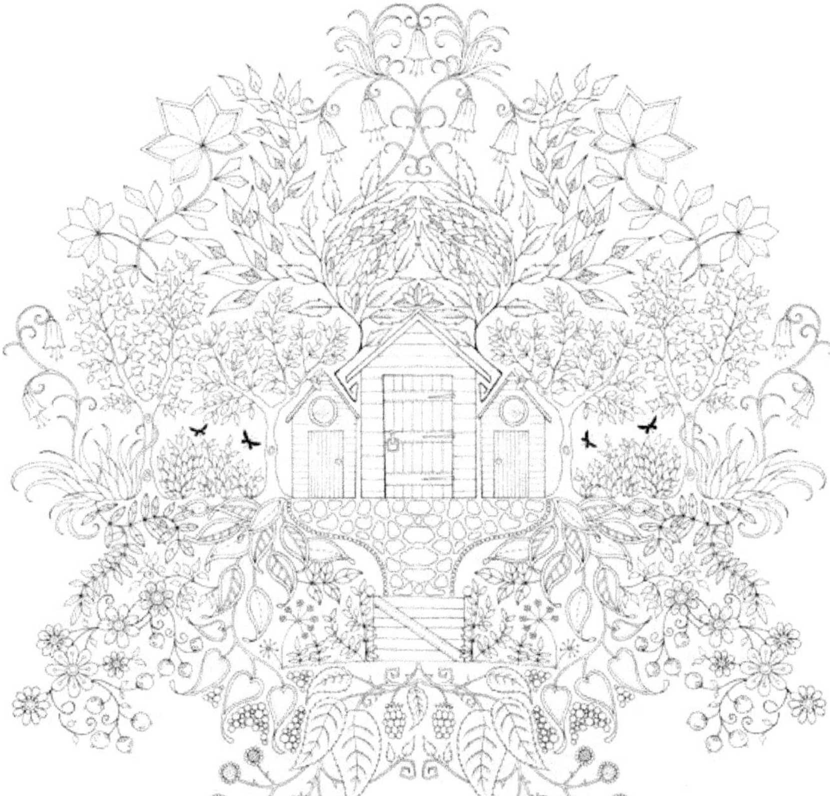

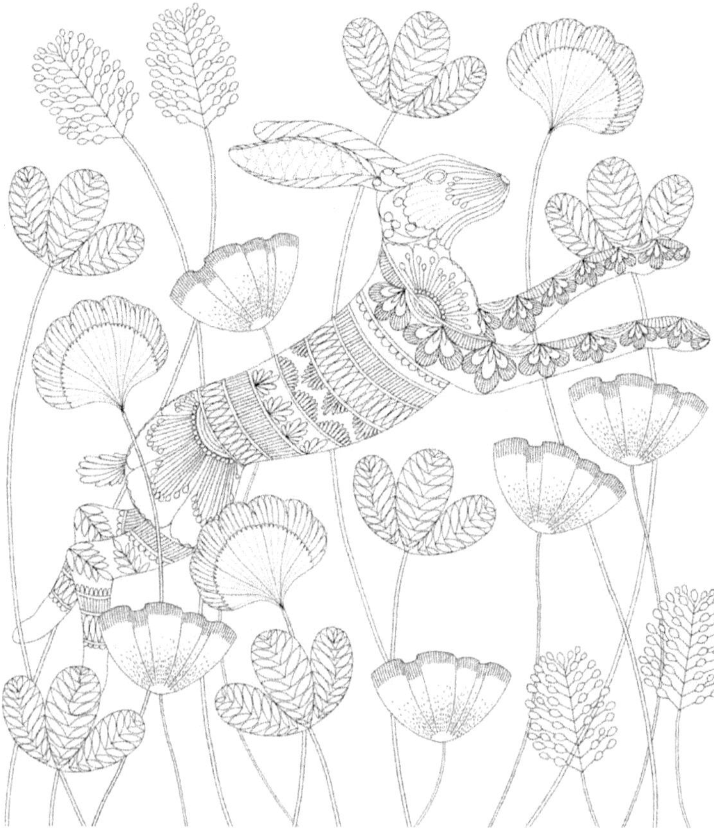

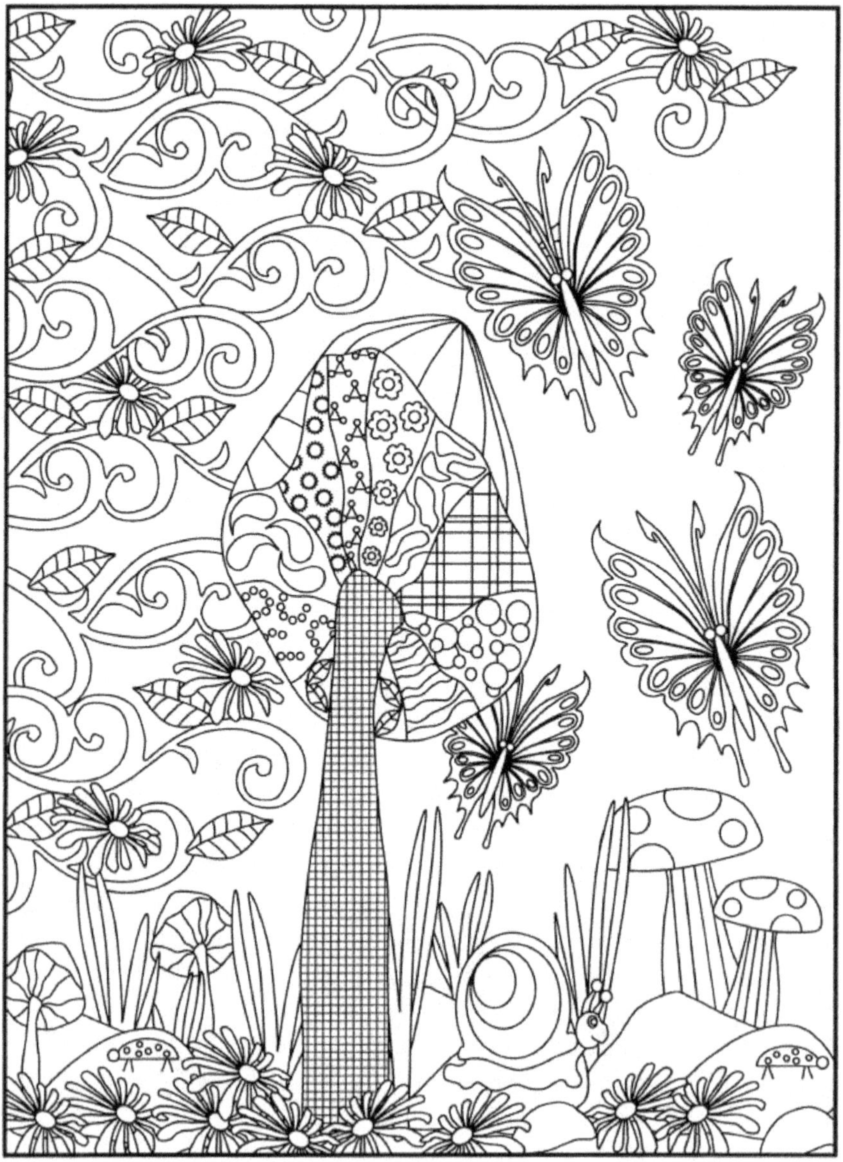

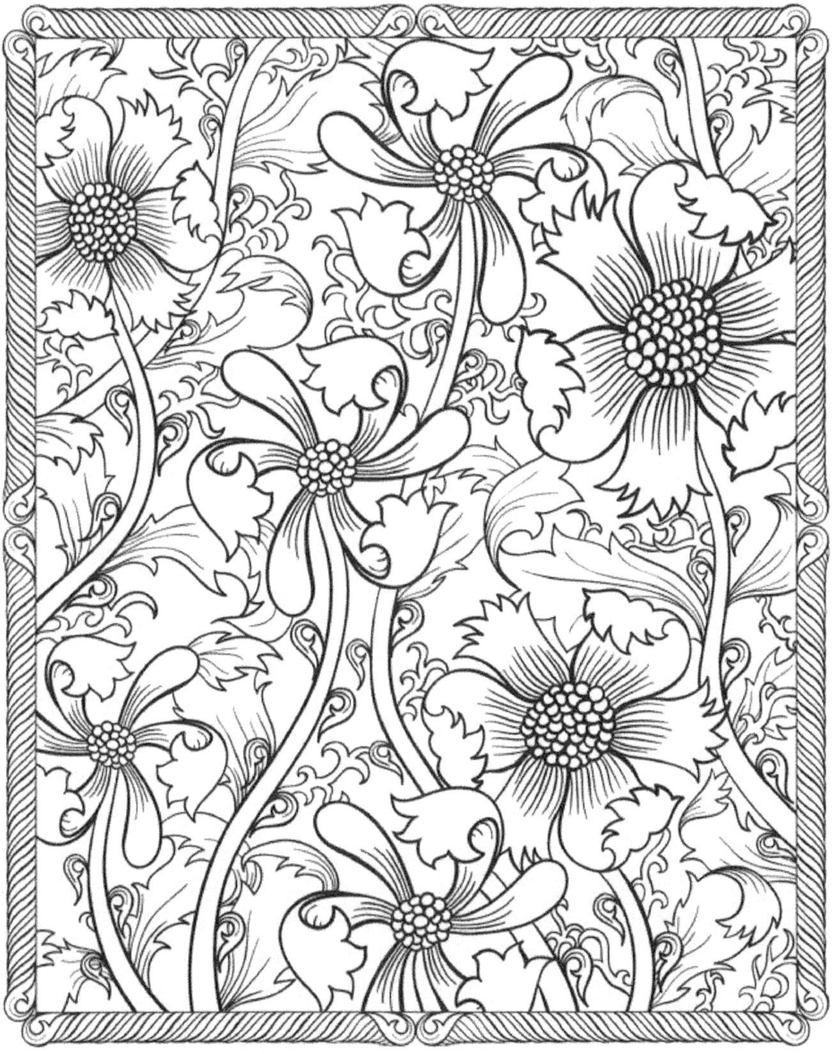

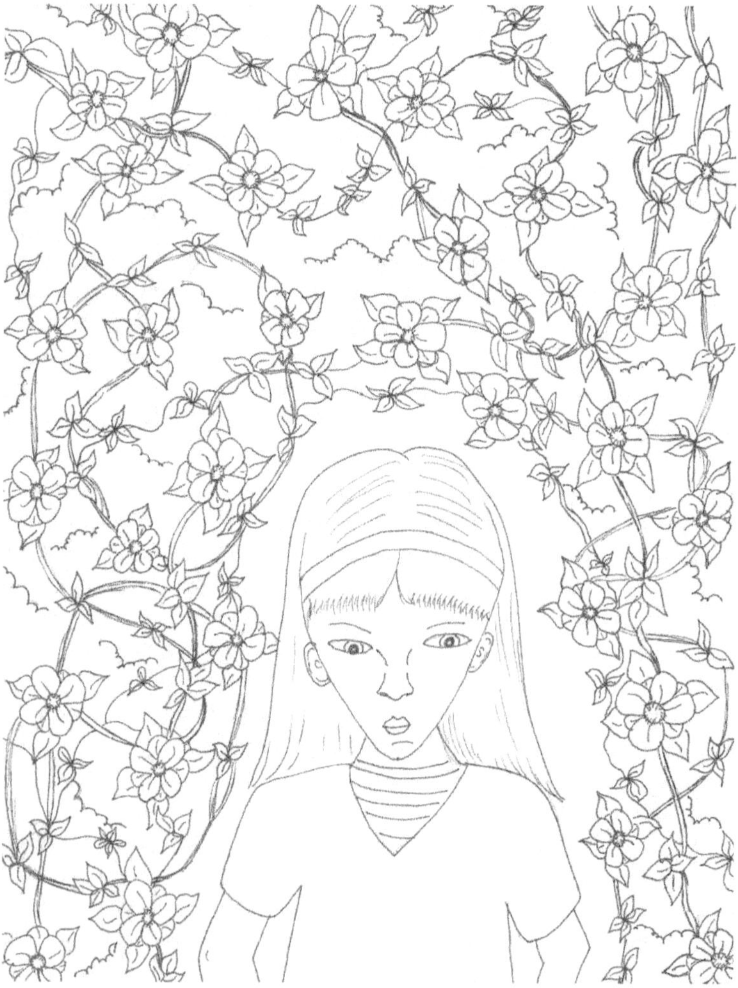

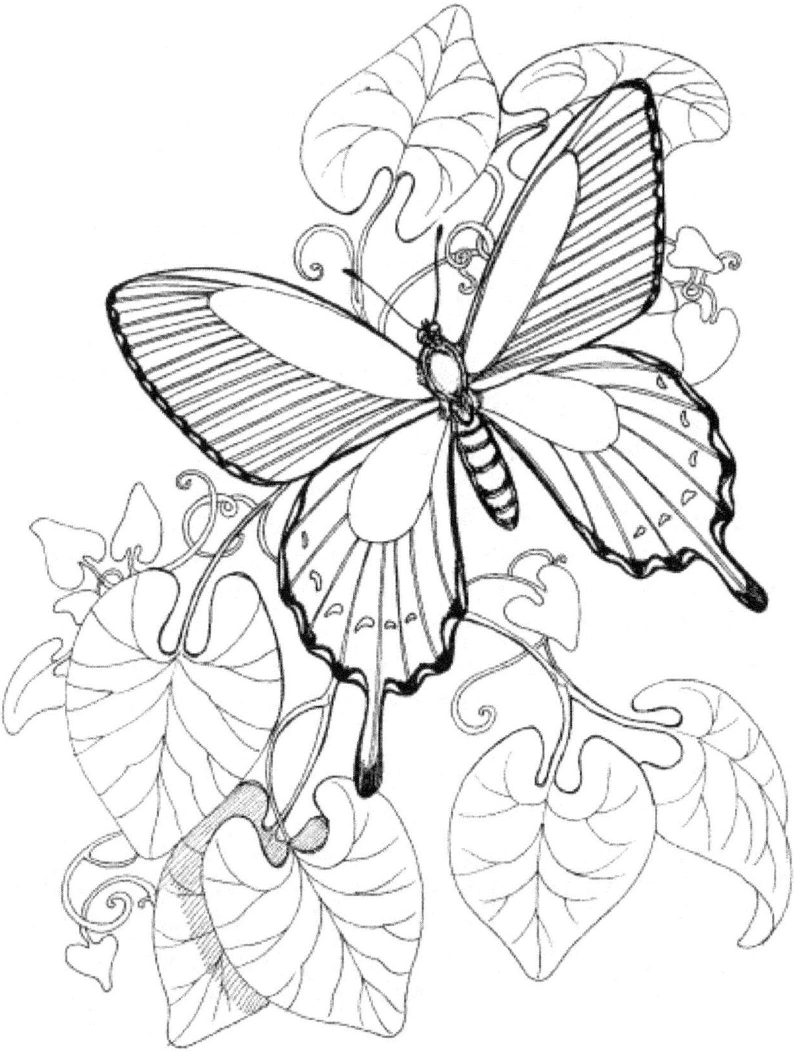

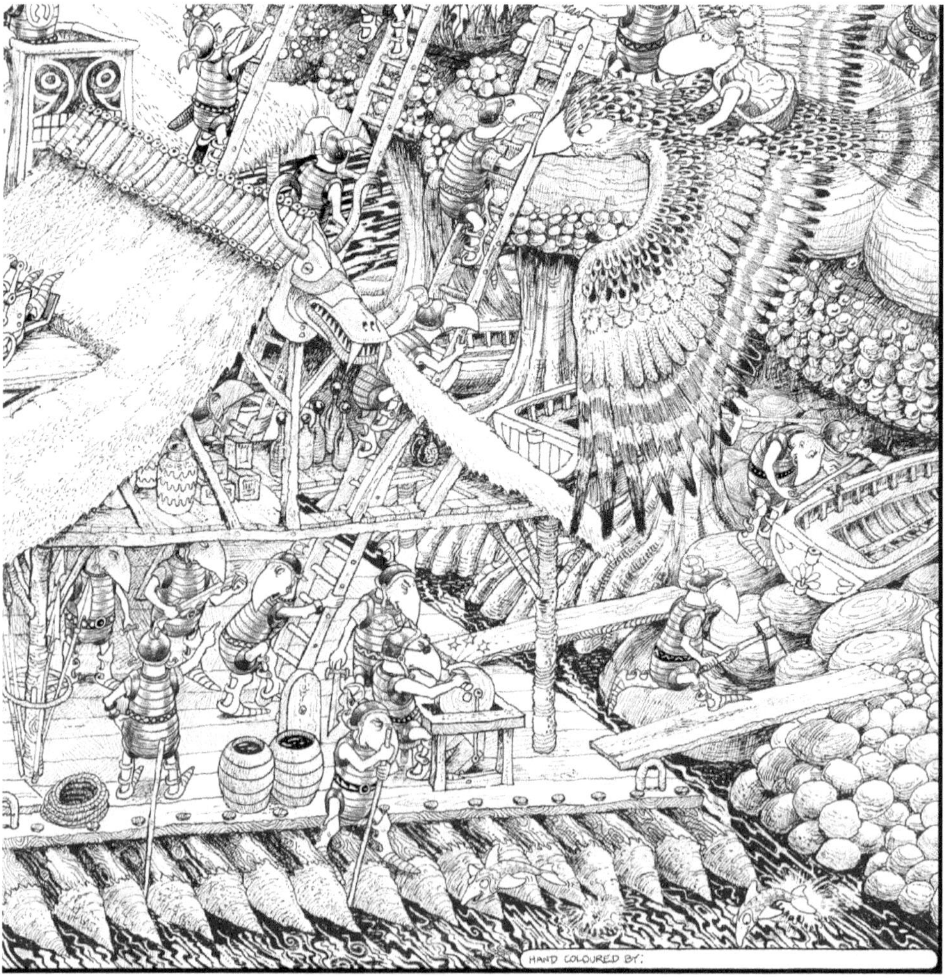
HAND COLOURED BY:

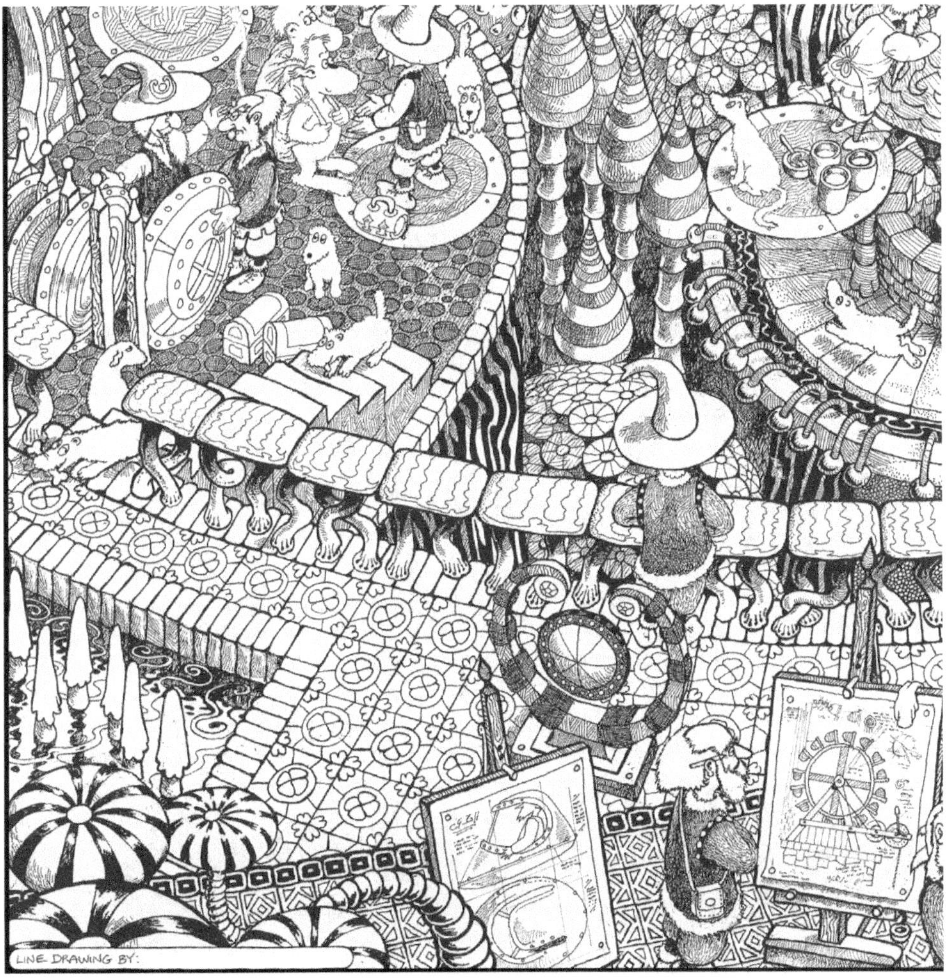
LINE DRAWING BY:

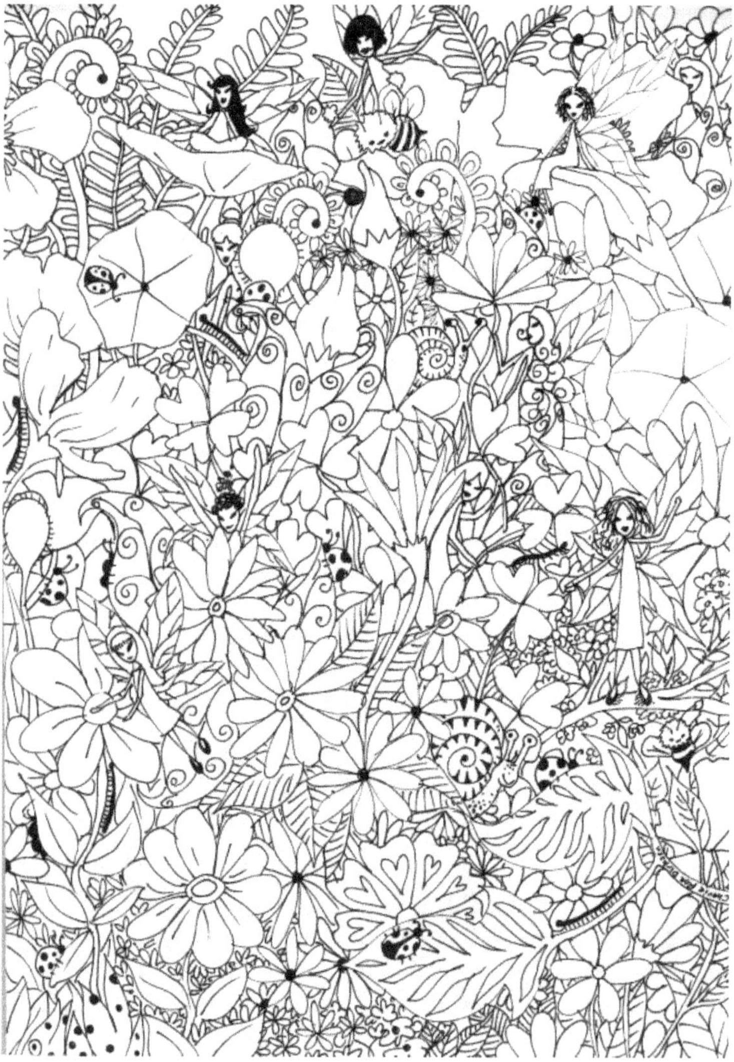

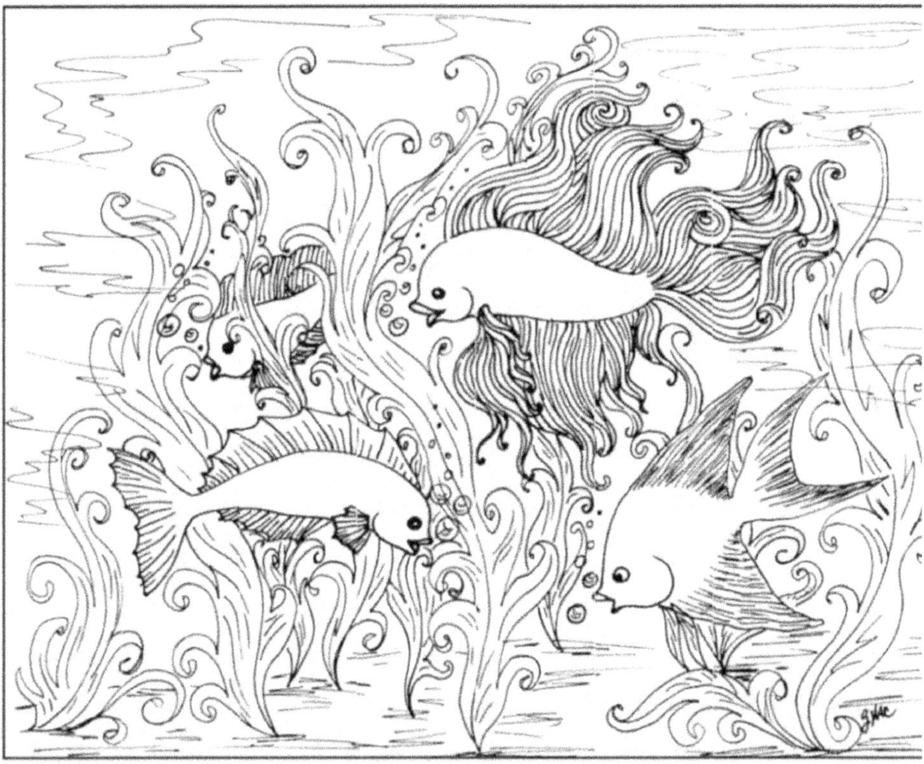

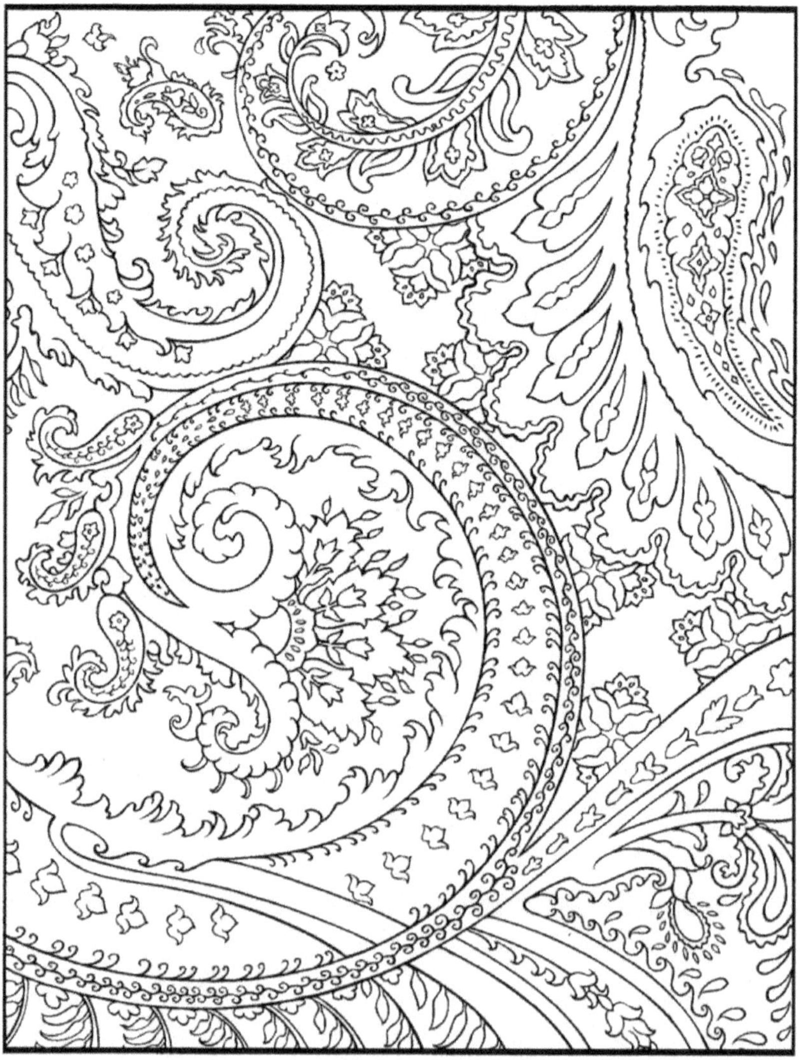

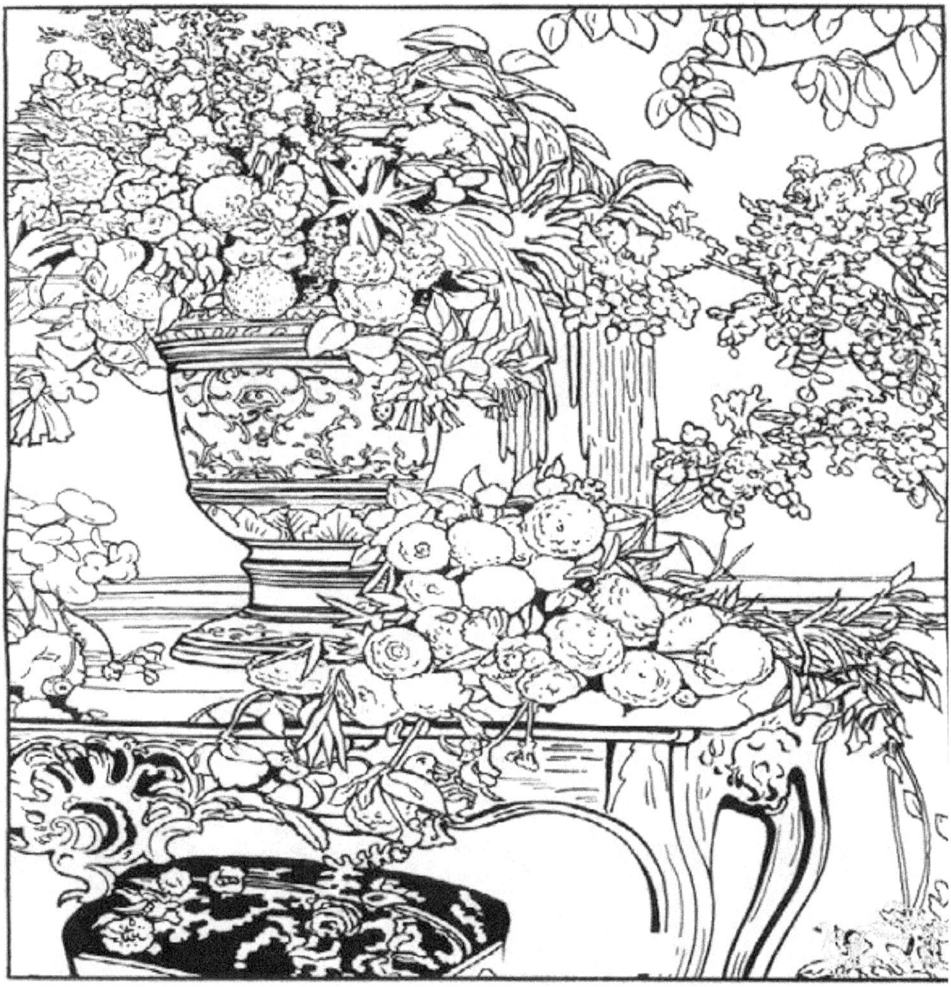

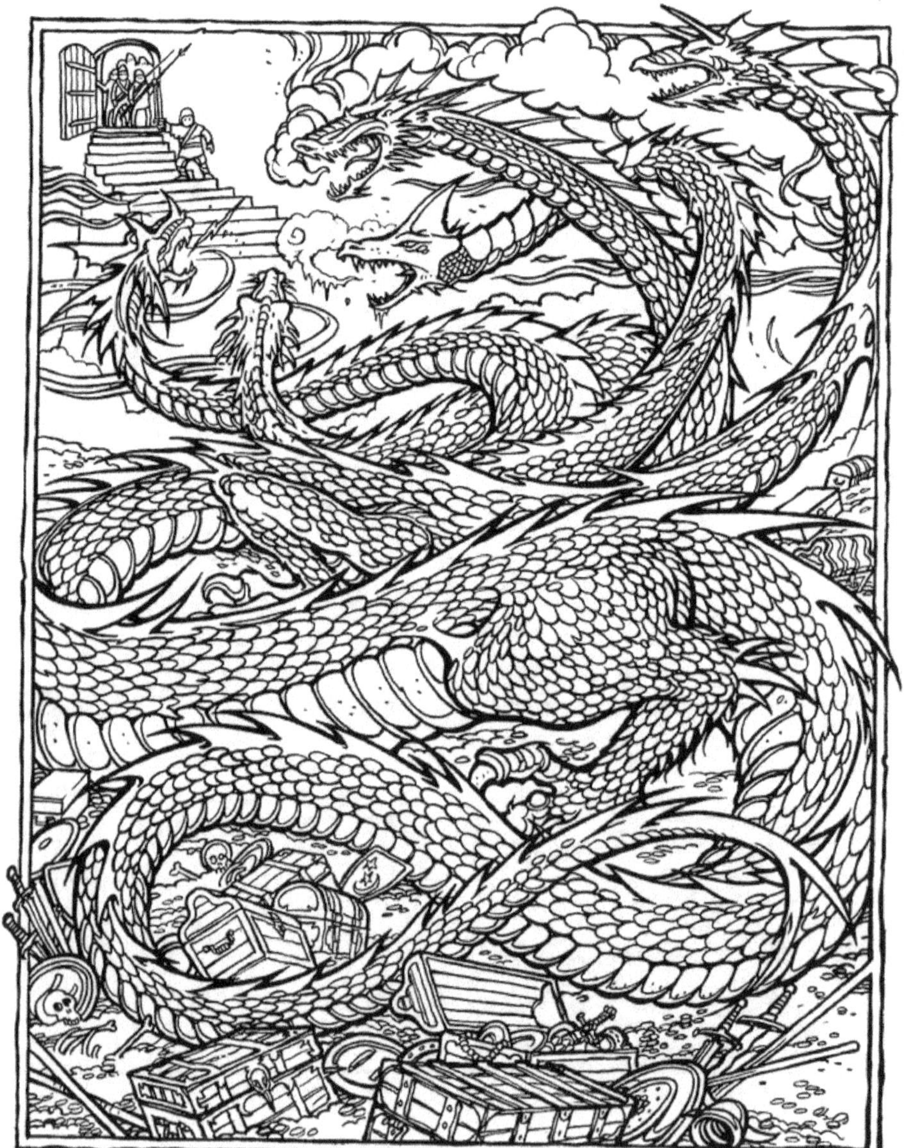

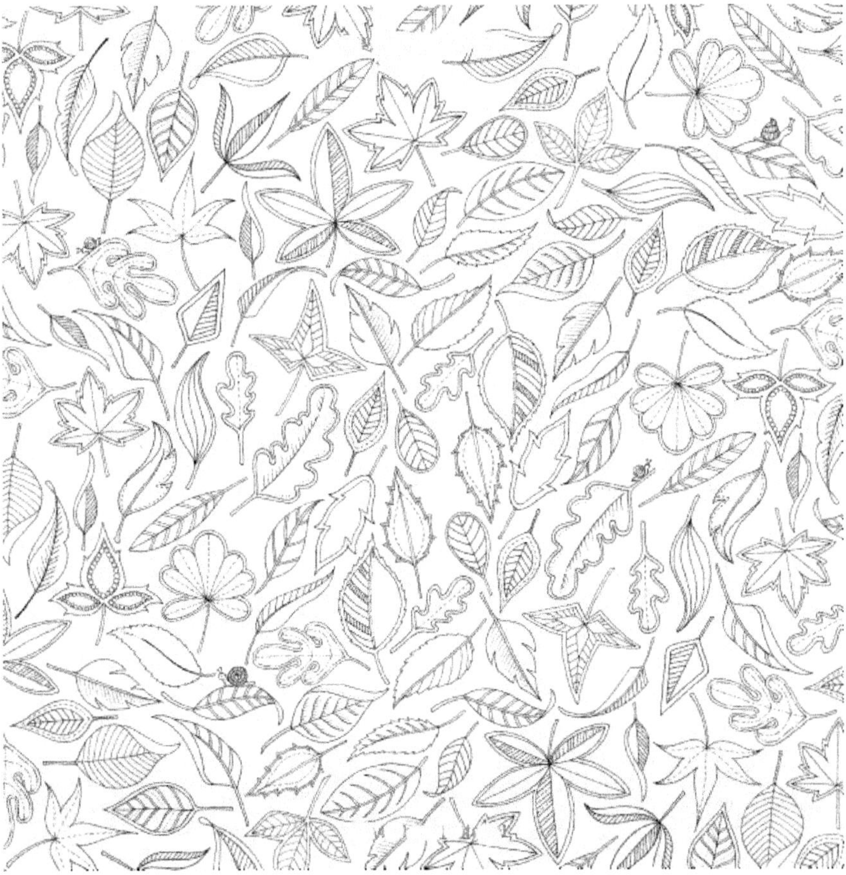

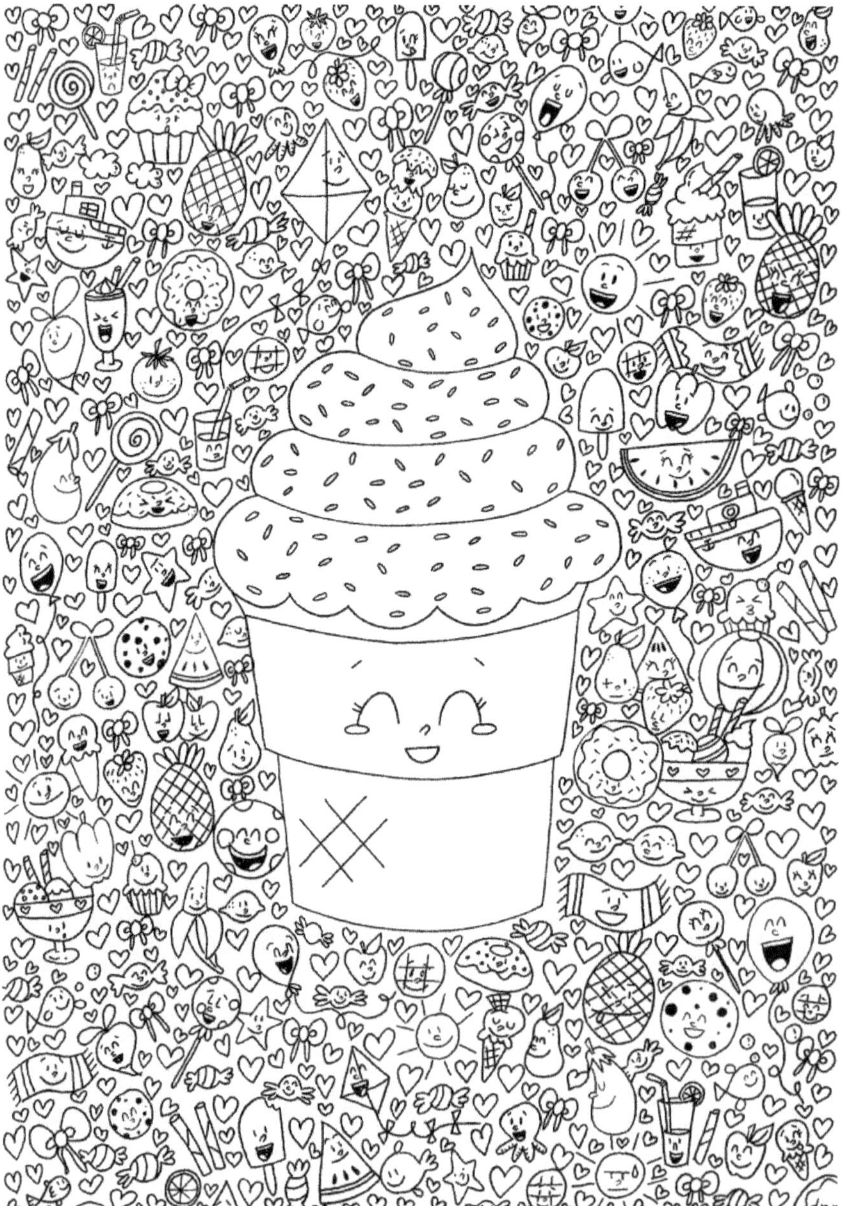
dpr

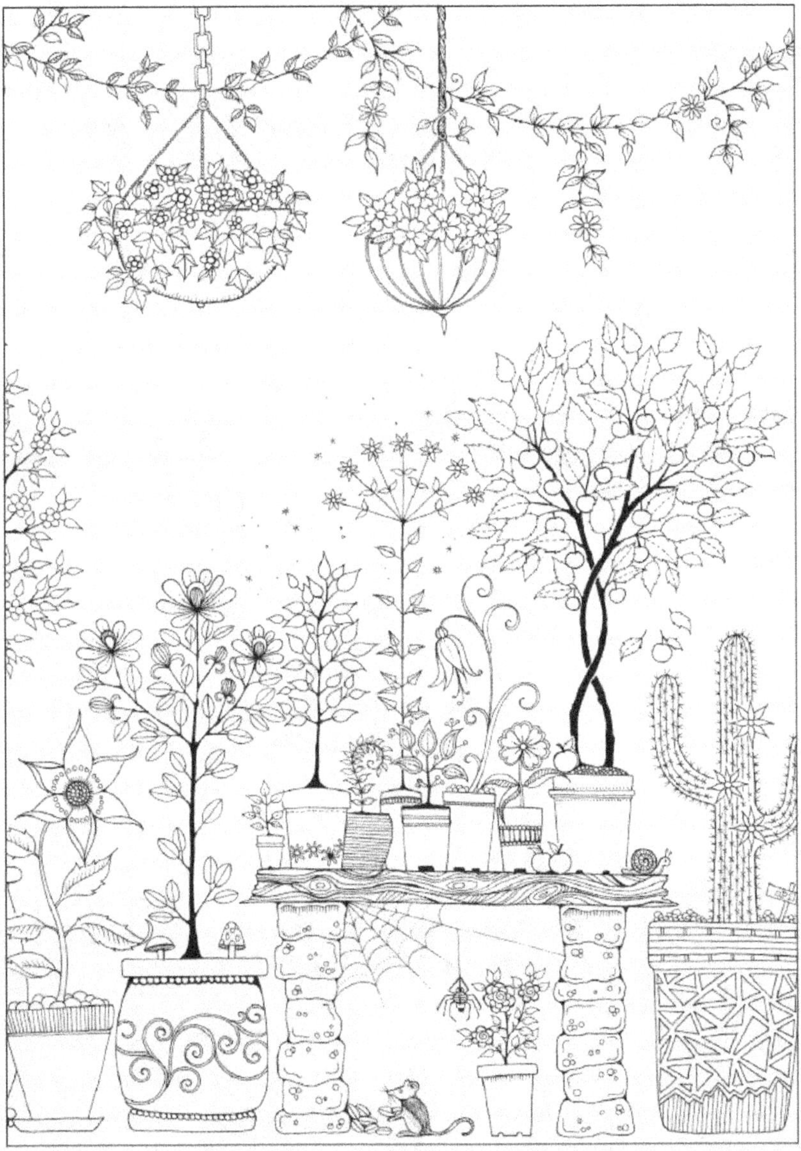

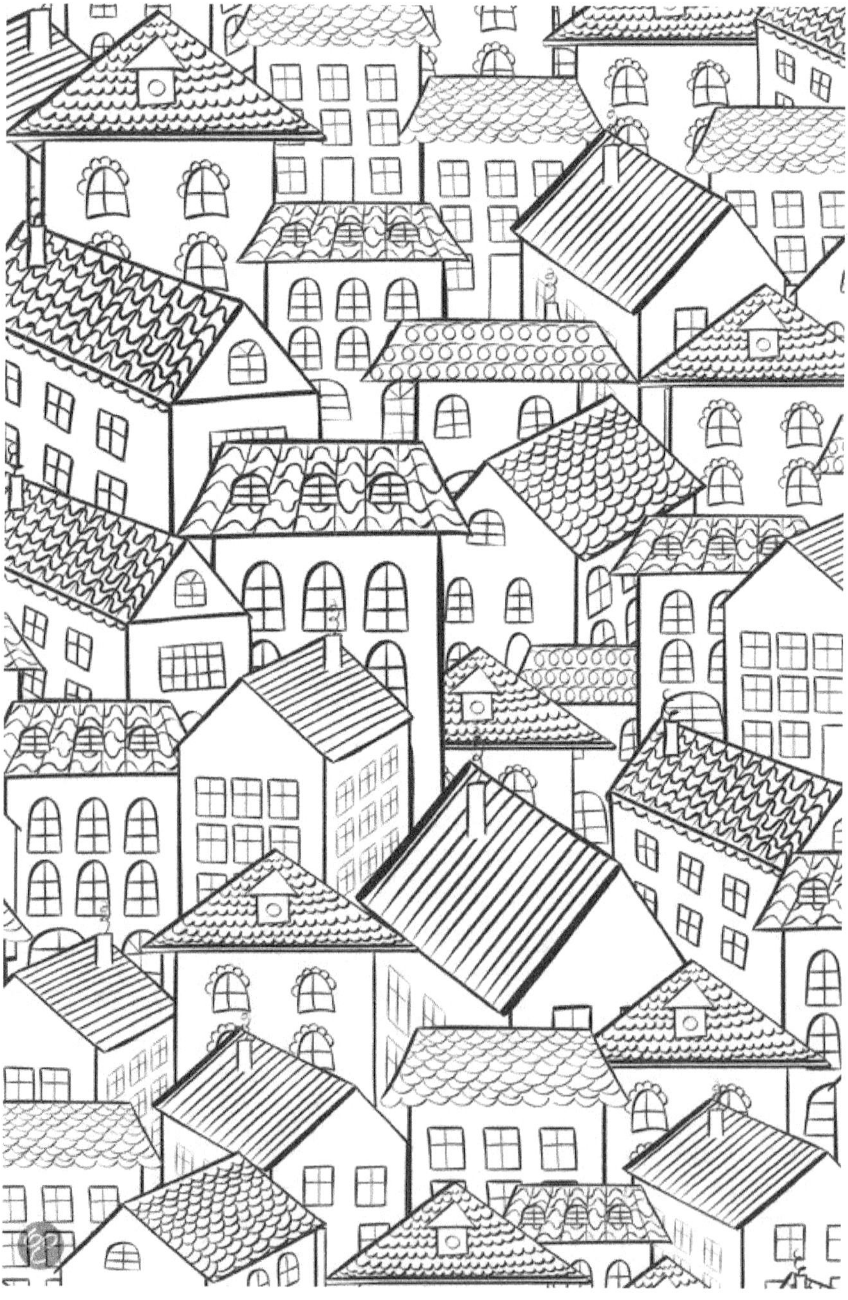

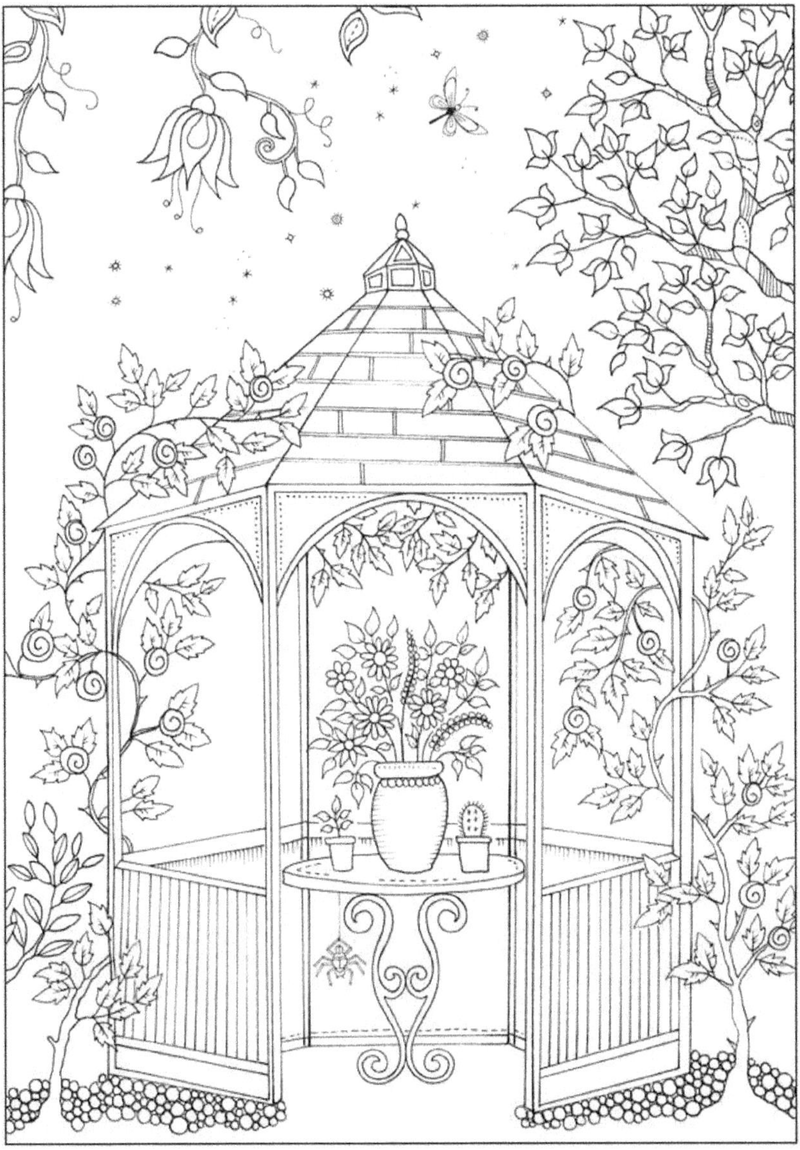

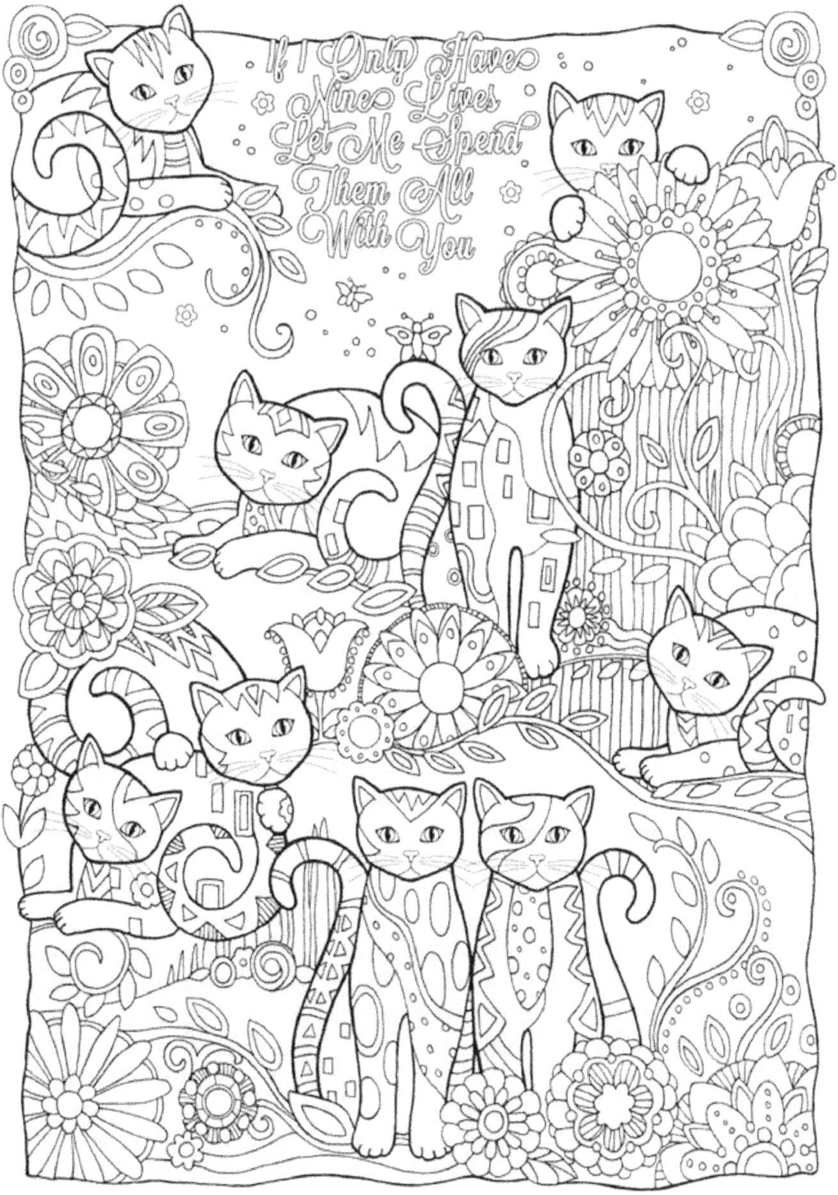
If I Only Have Nine Lives Let Me Spend Them All With You

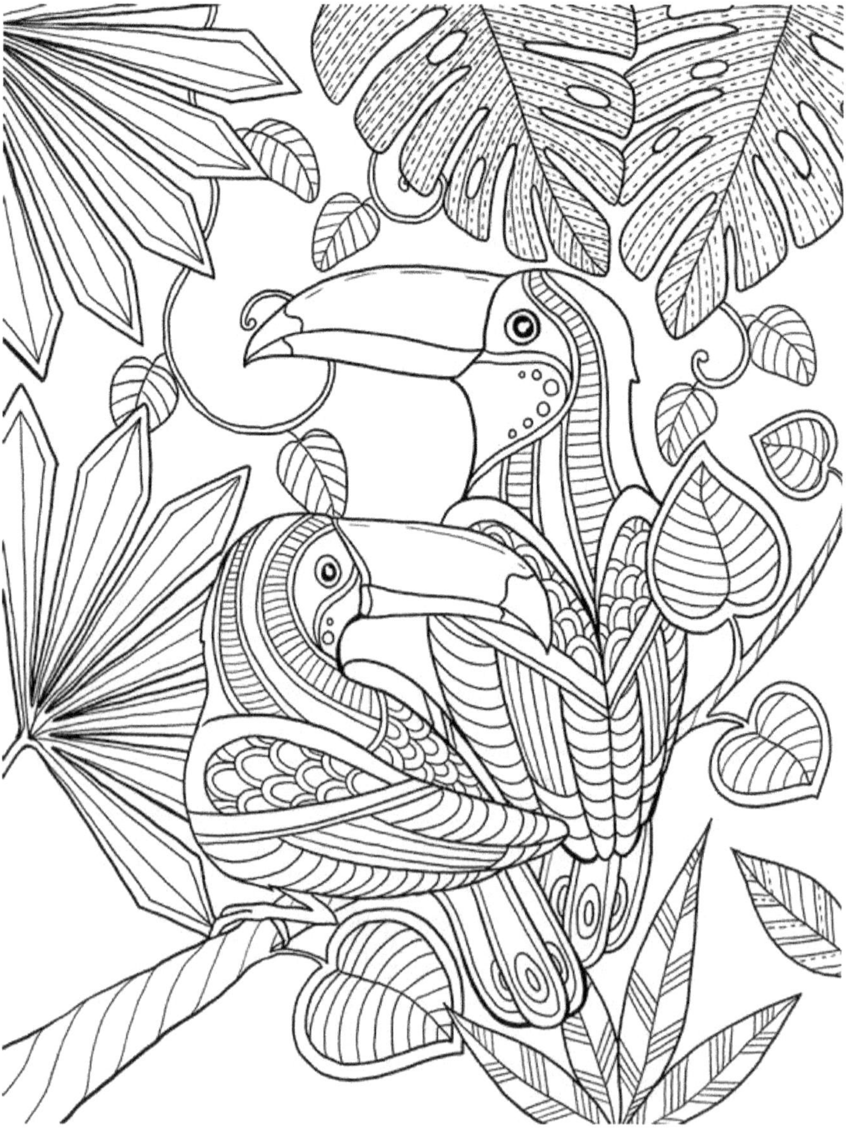

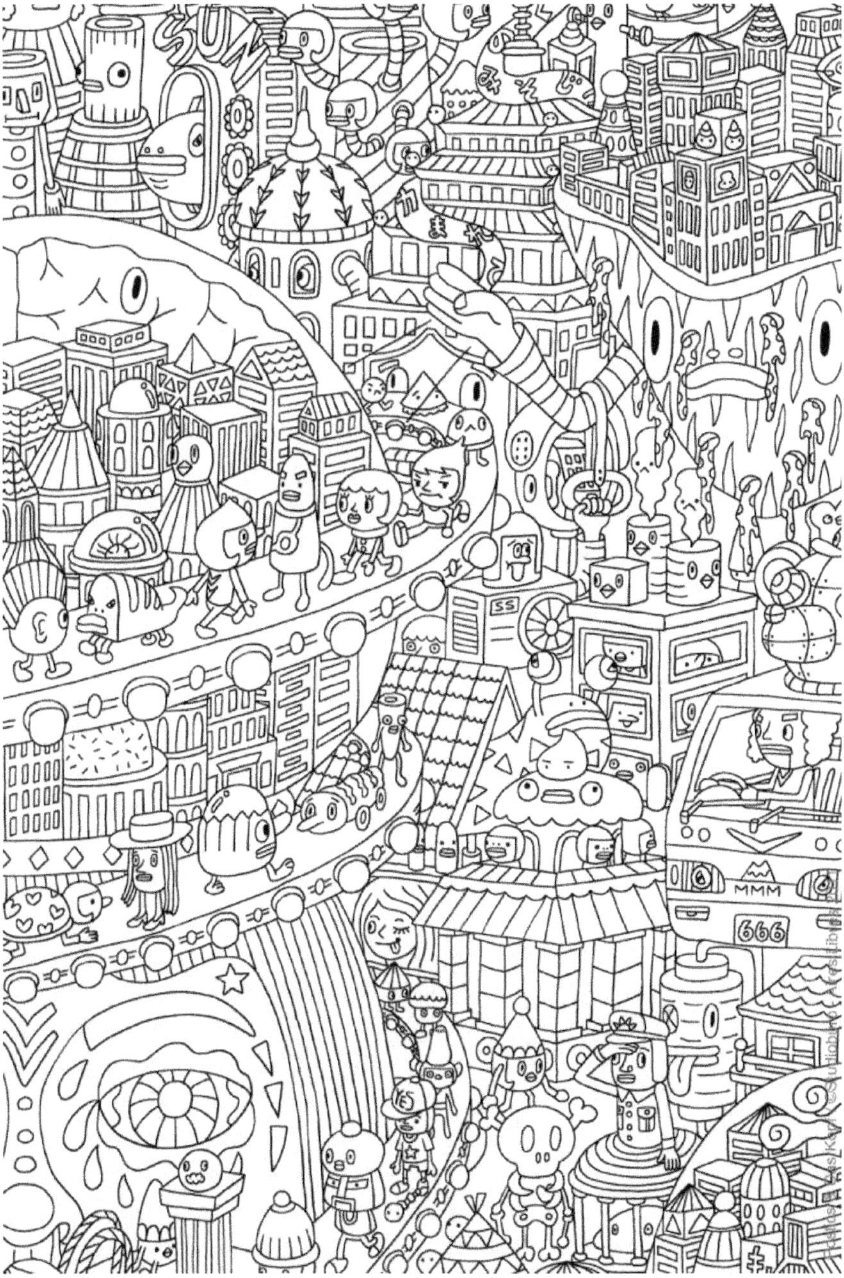
SUN
SS
MMM
666

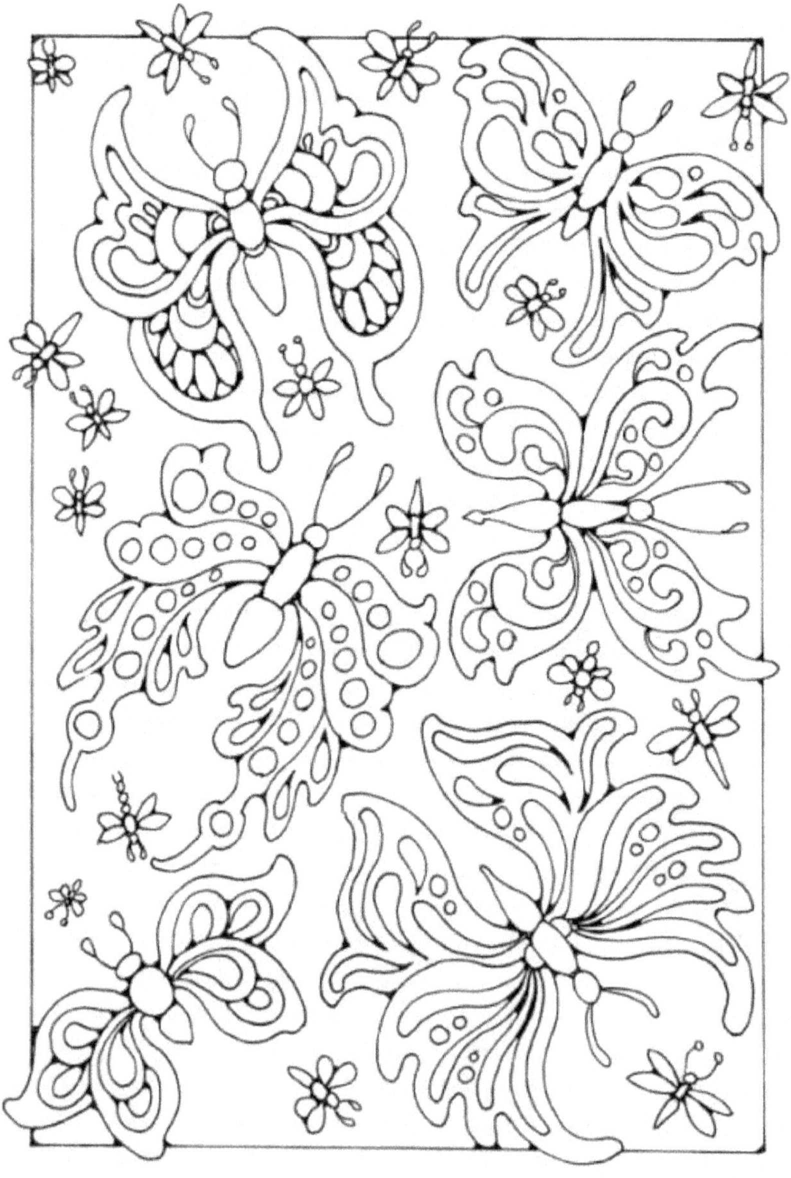

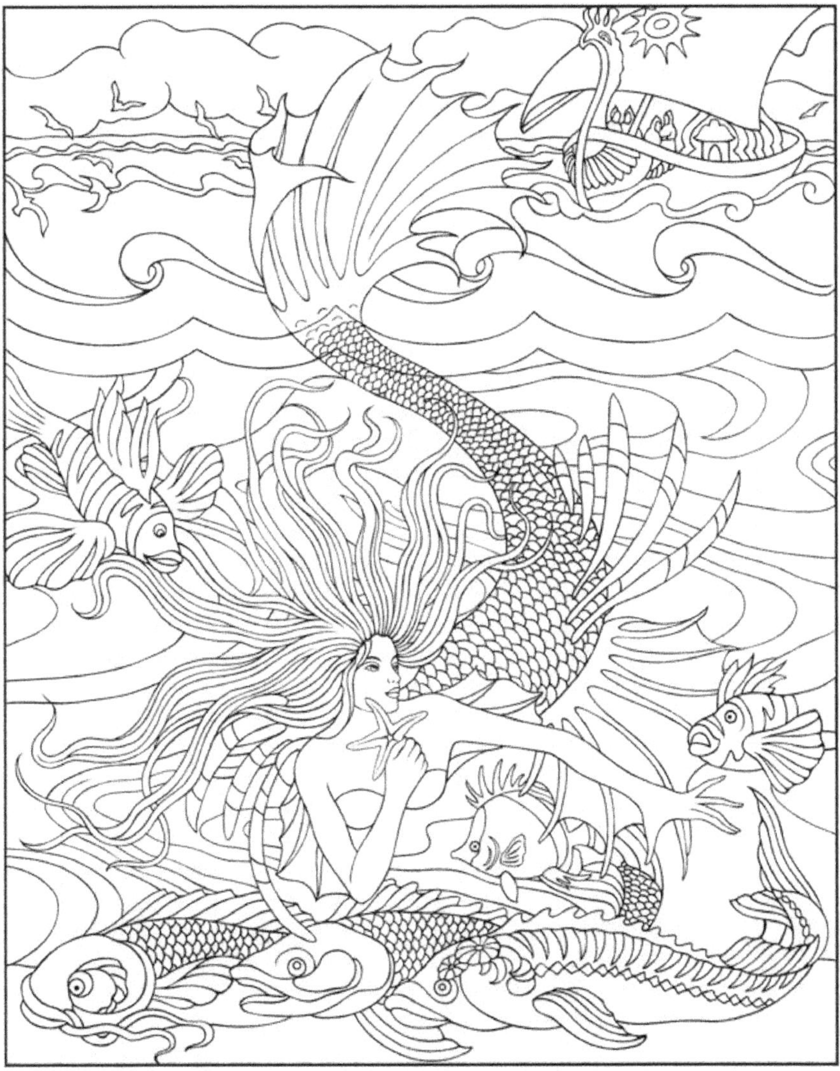

In this story from the United Kingdom, a young man with a beautiful voice enchanted the ***Mermaid of Zennor*** with his songs. He then left the land to live with her under the waters.

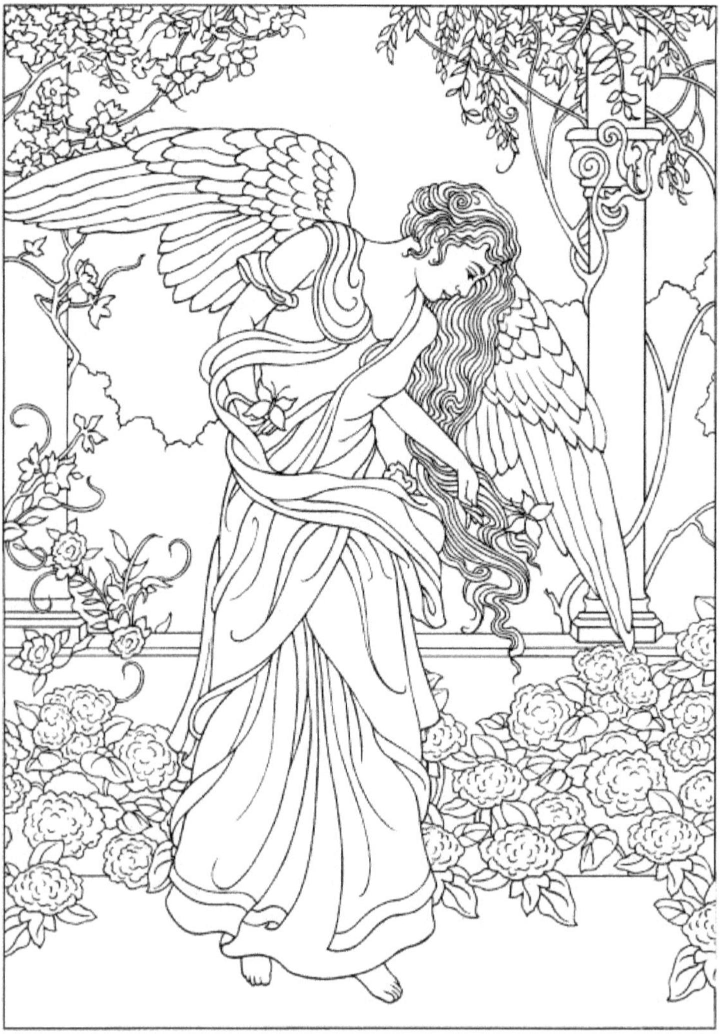

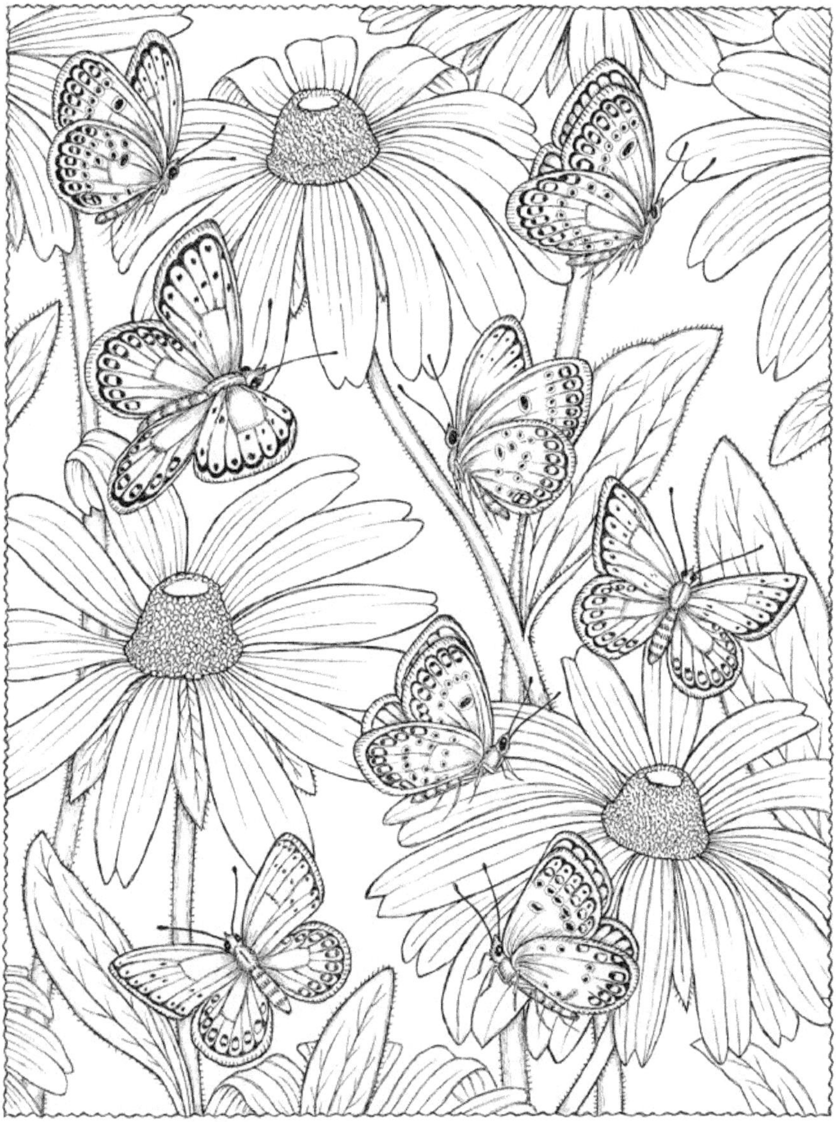

Blue butterflies and black-eyed Susans

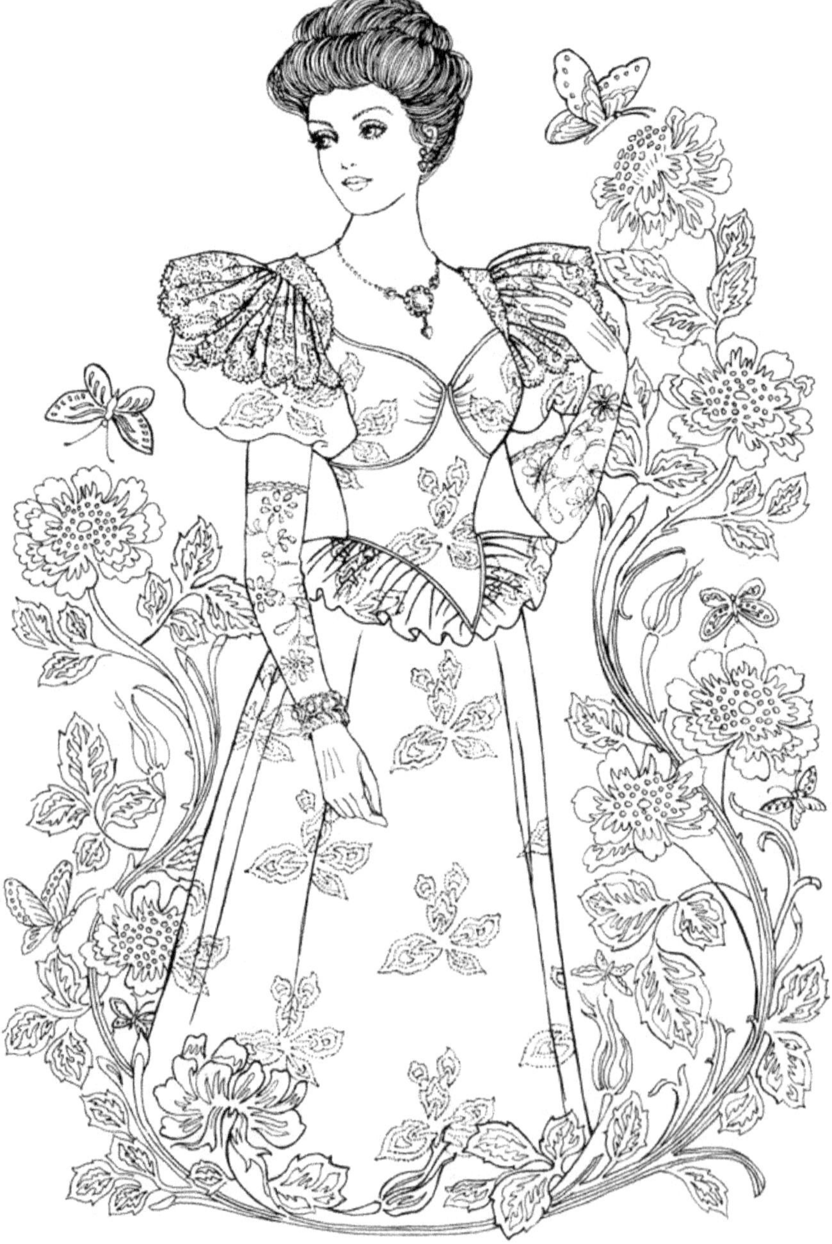

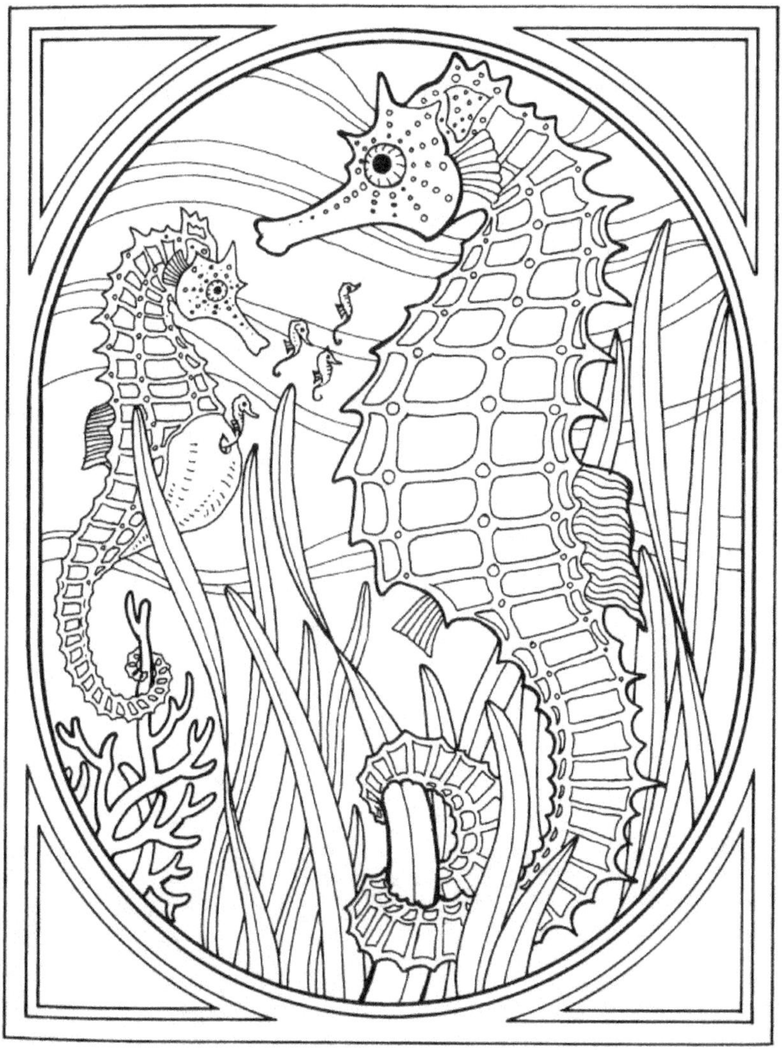

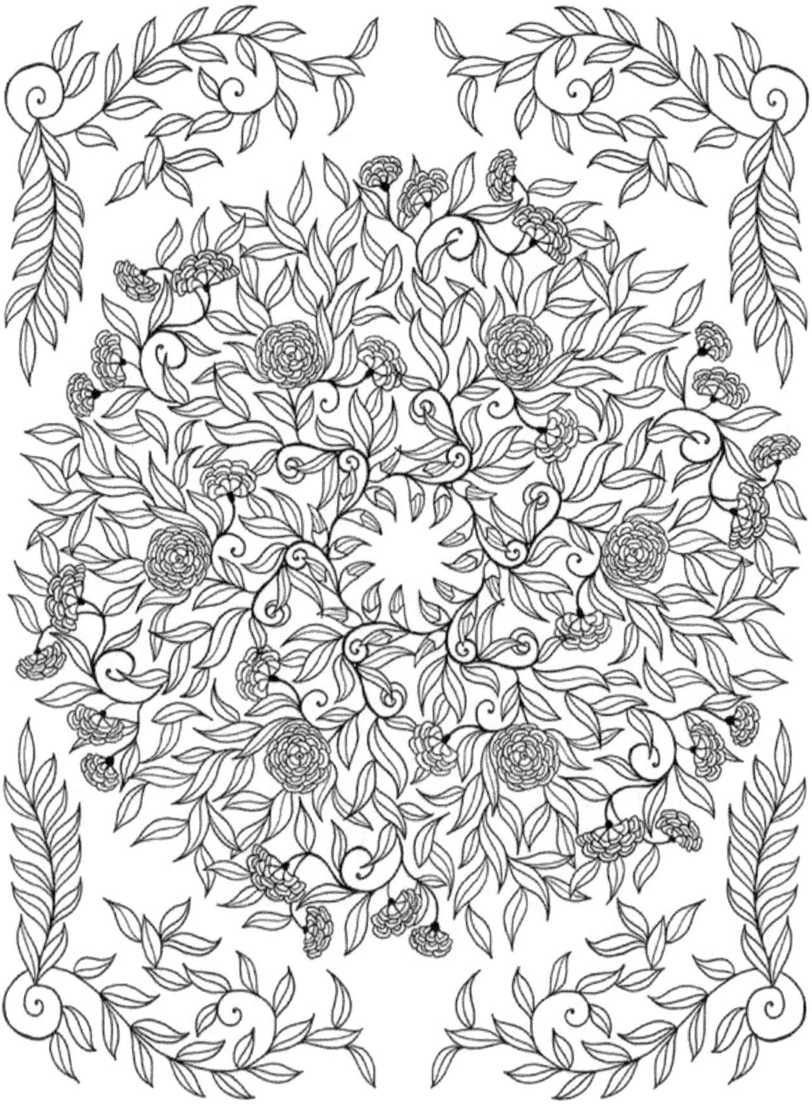

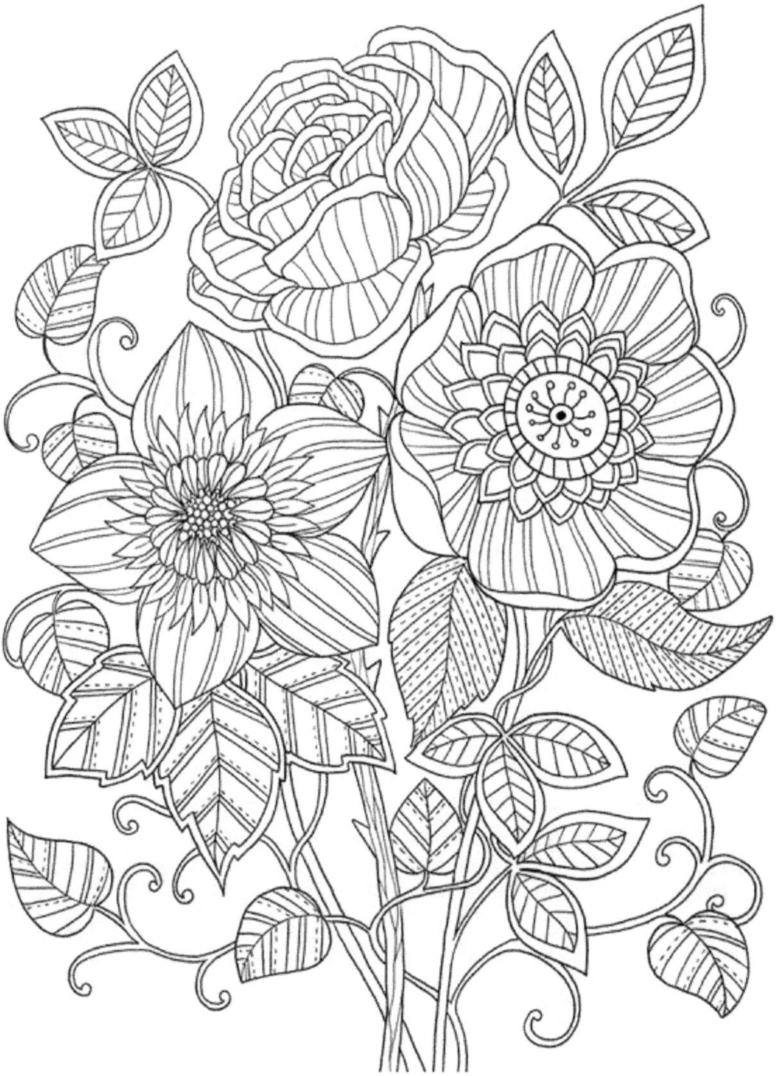

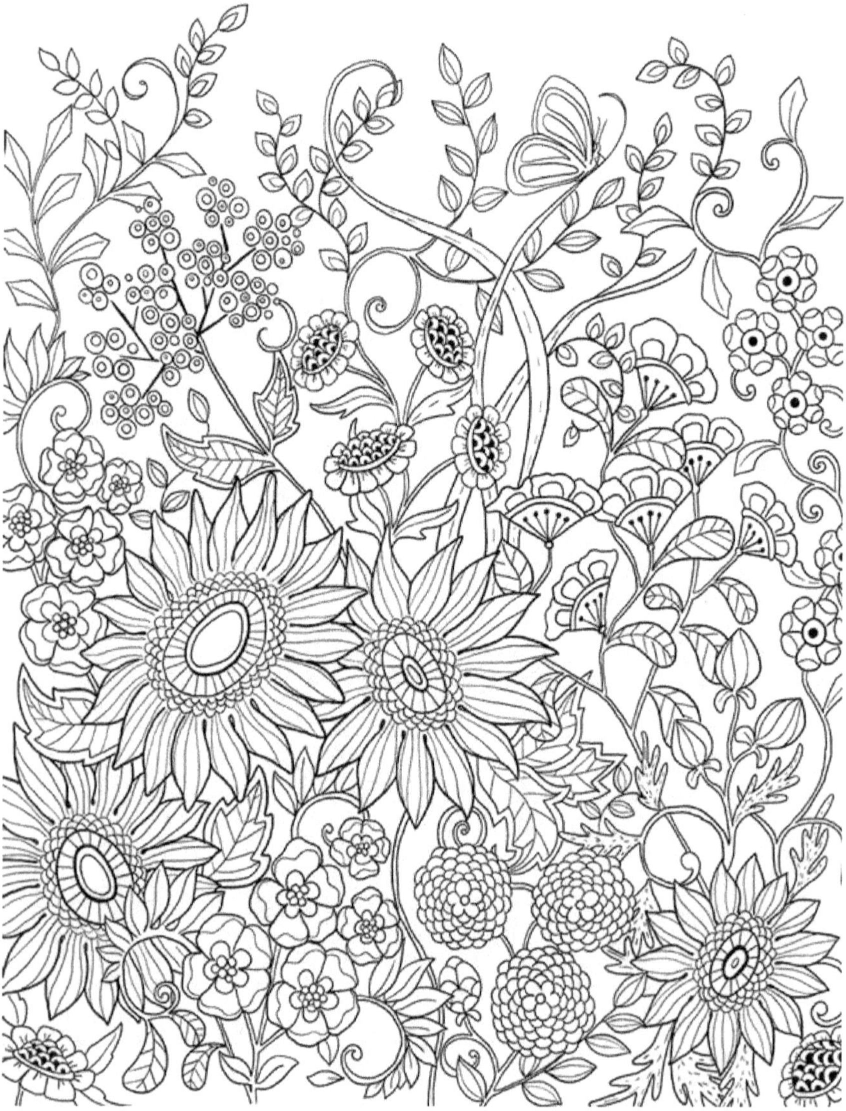

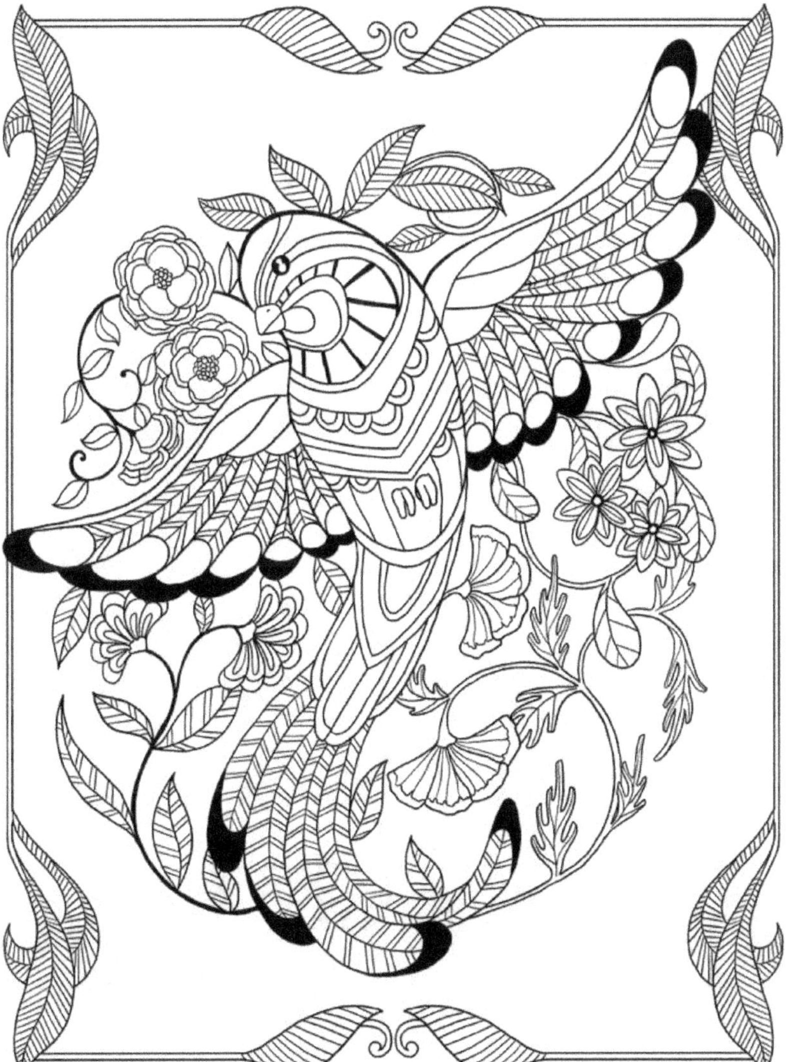

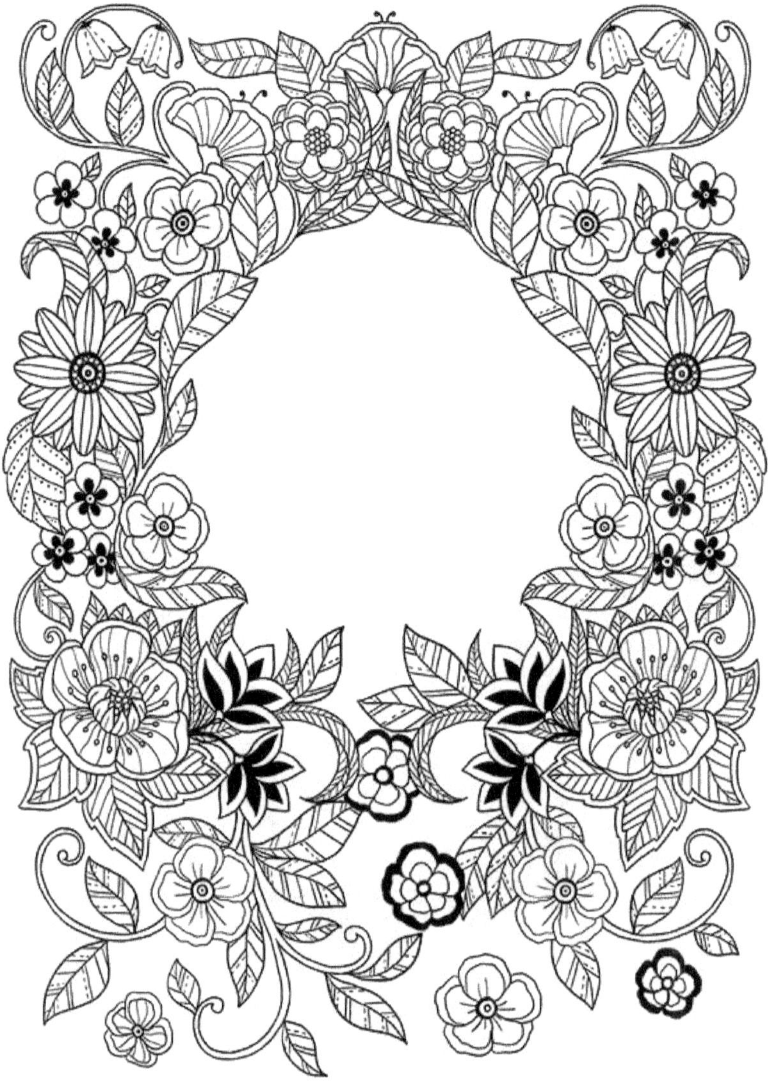

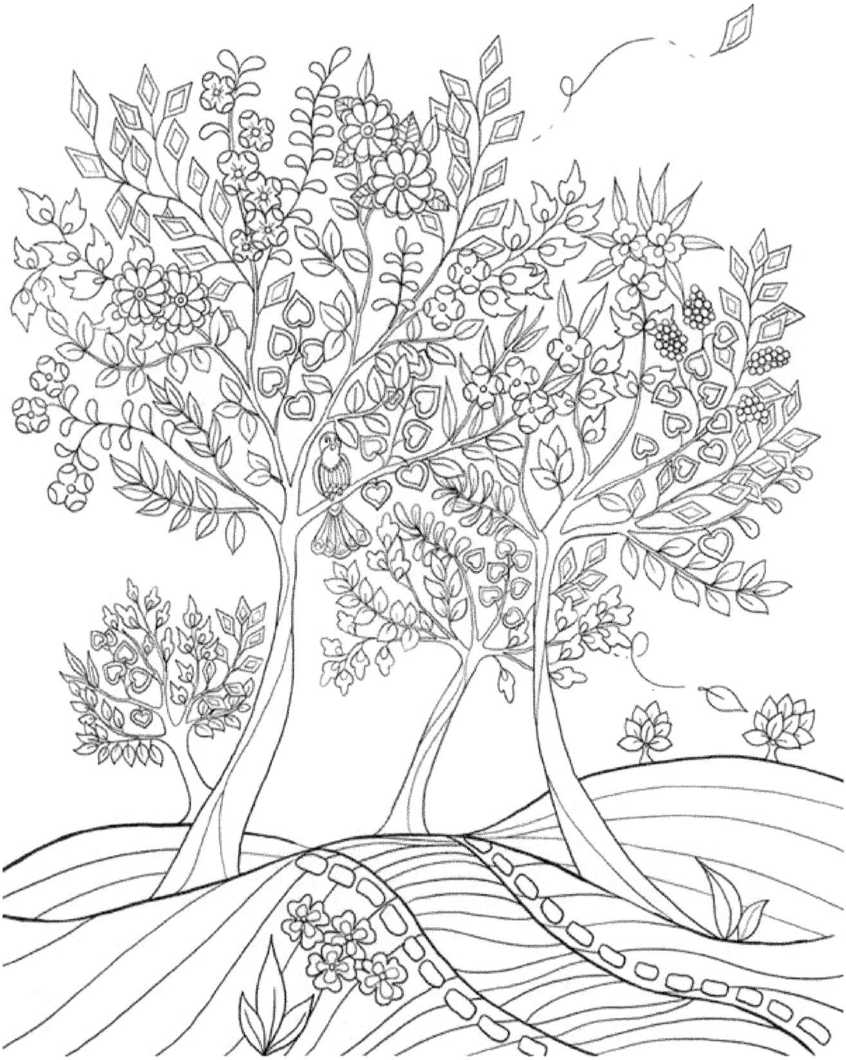

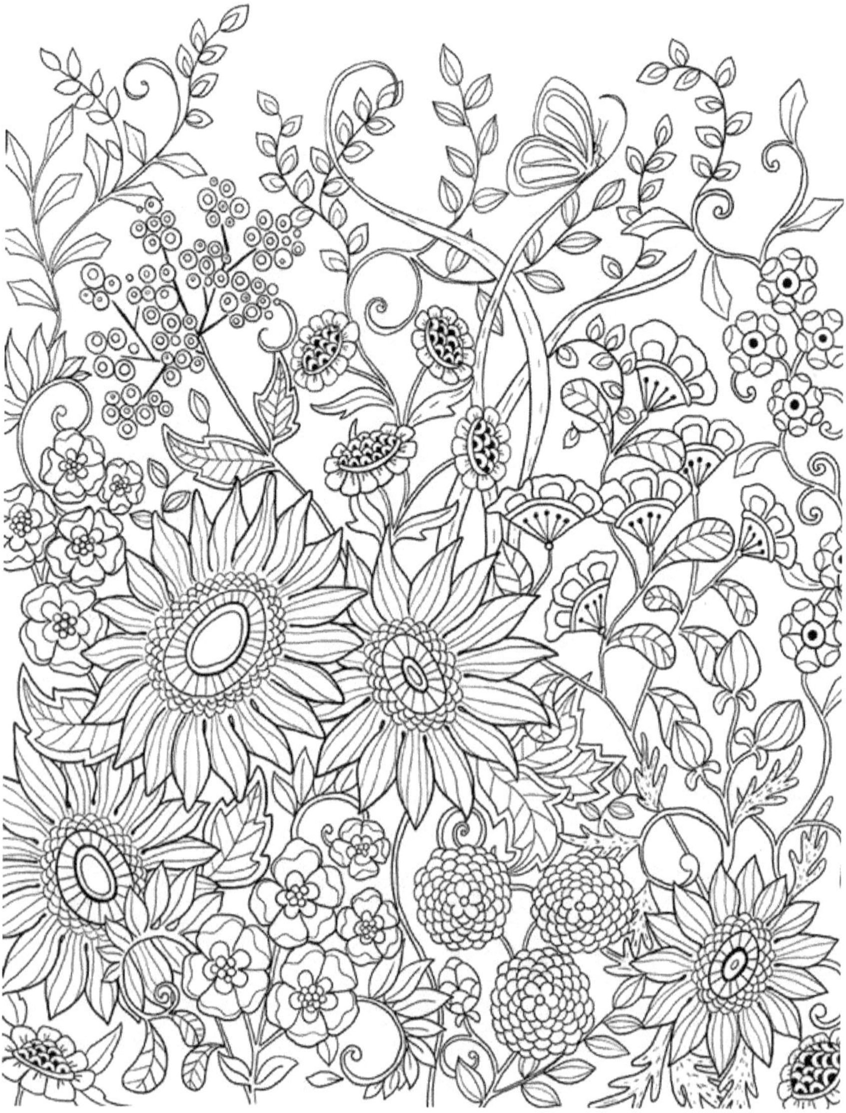

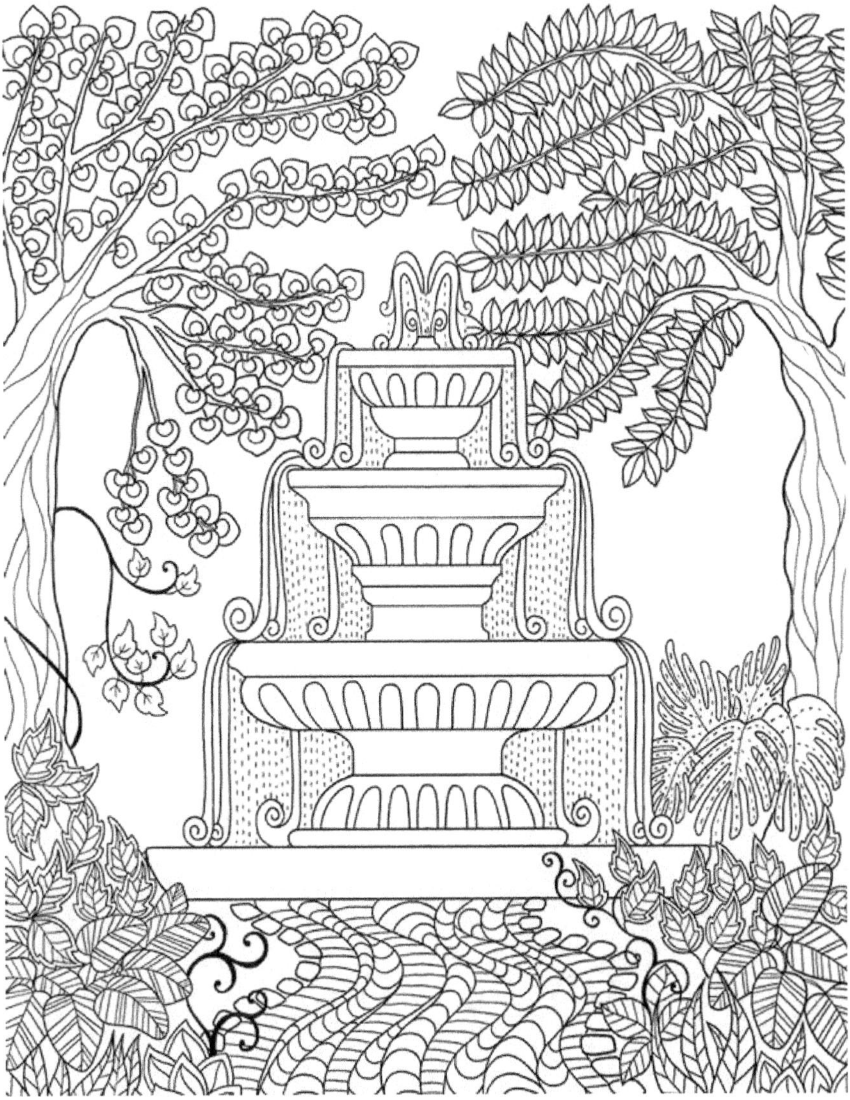

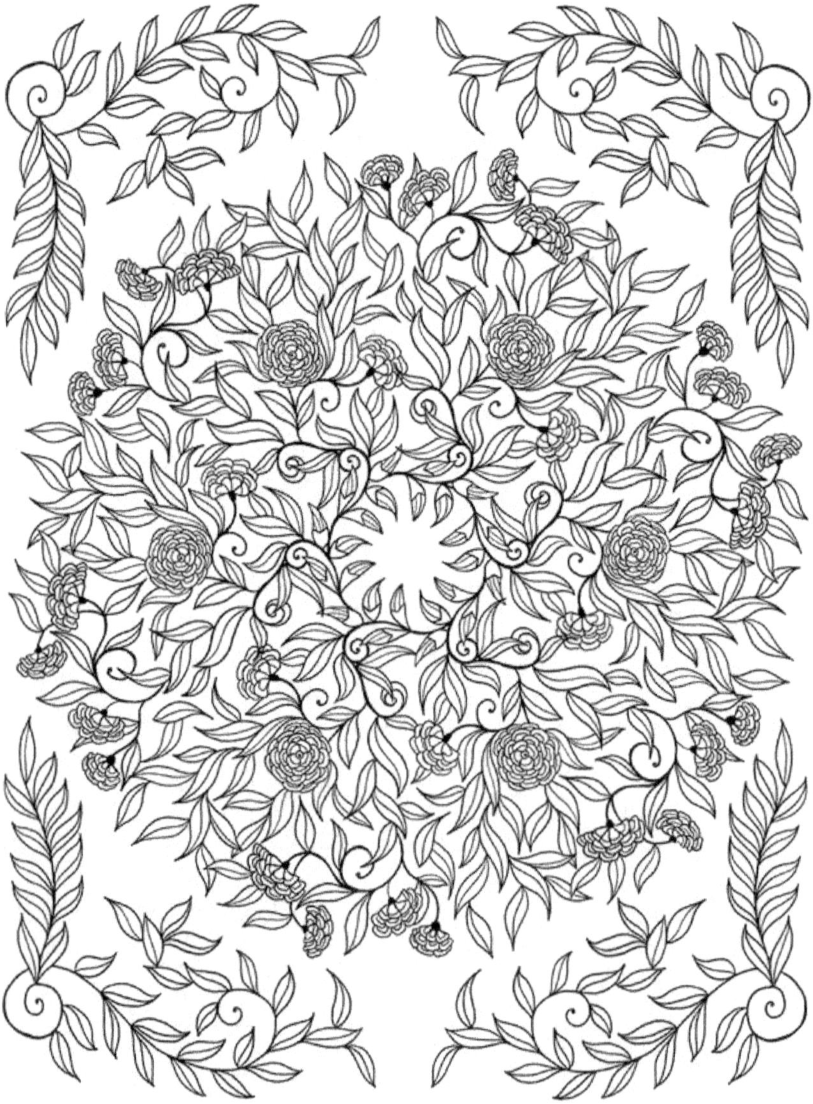

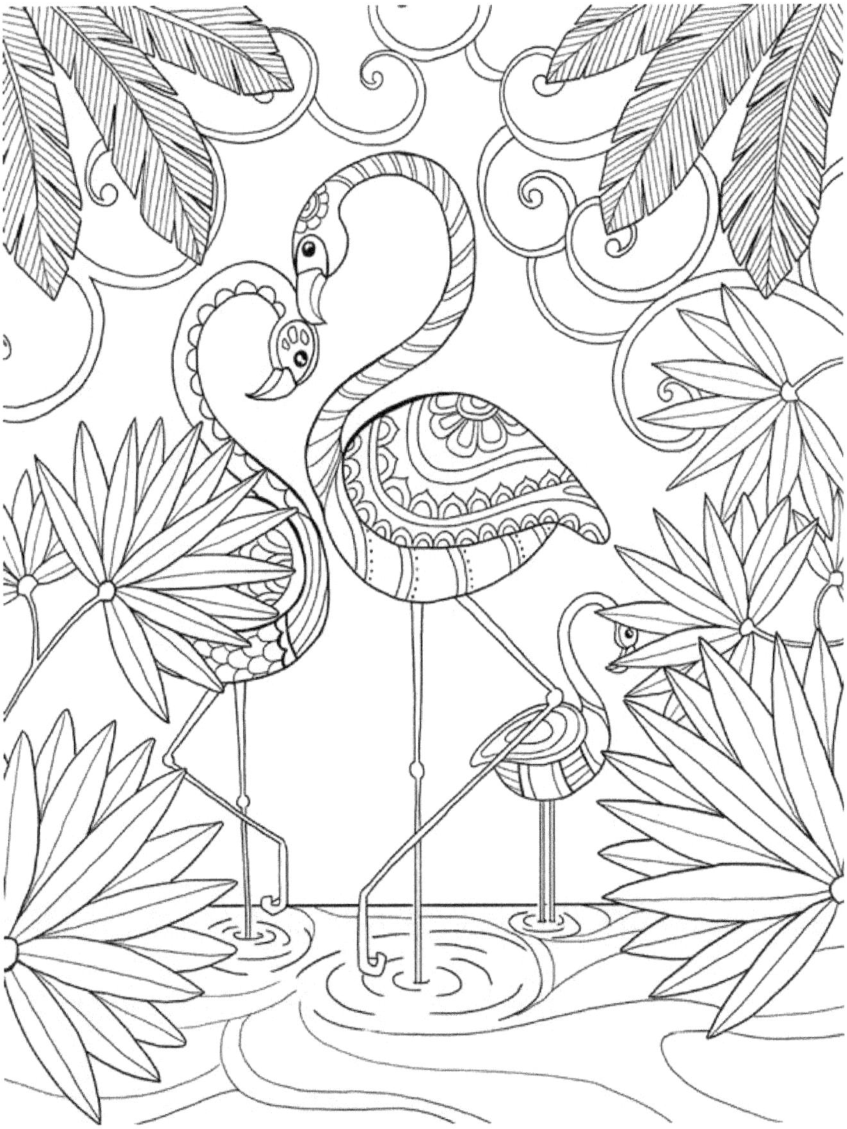

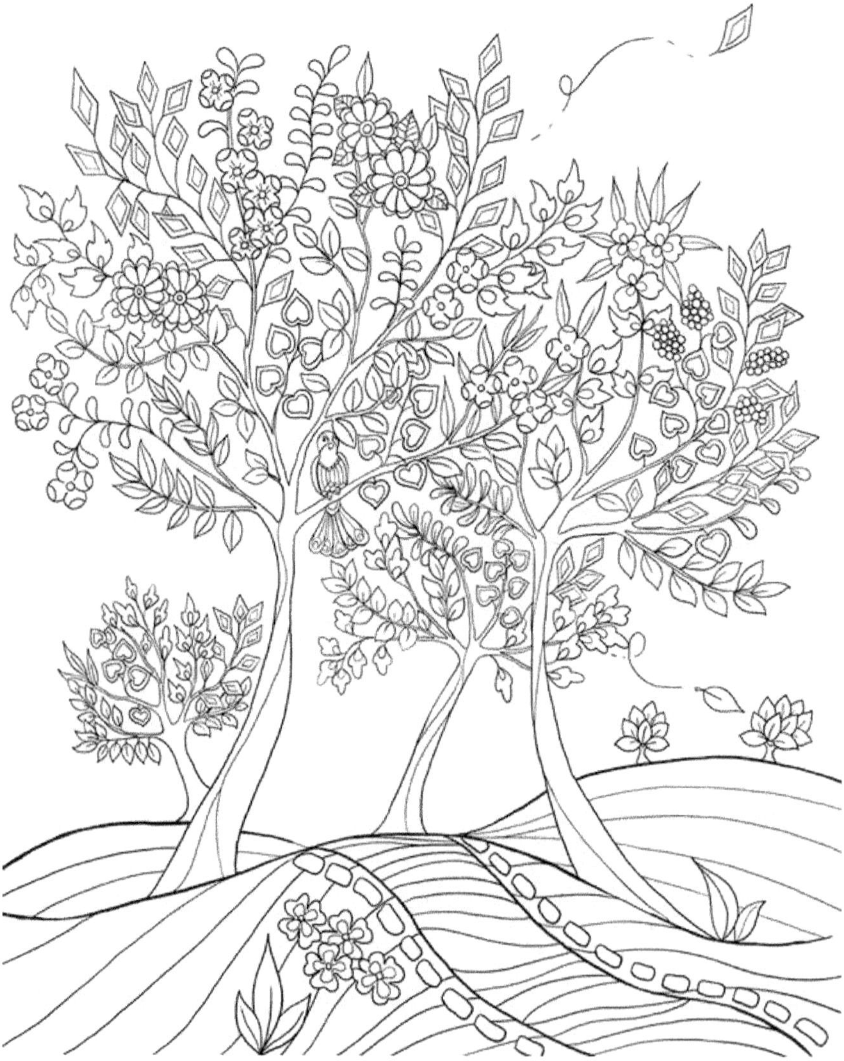

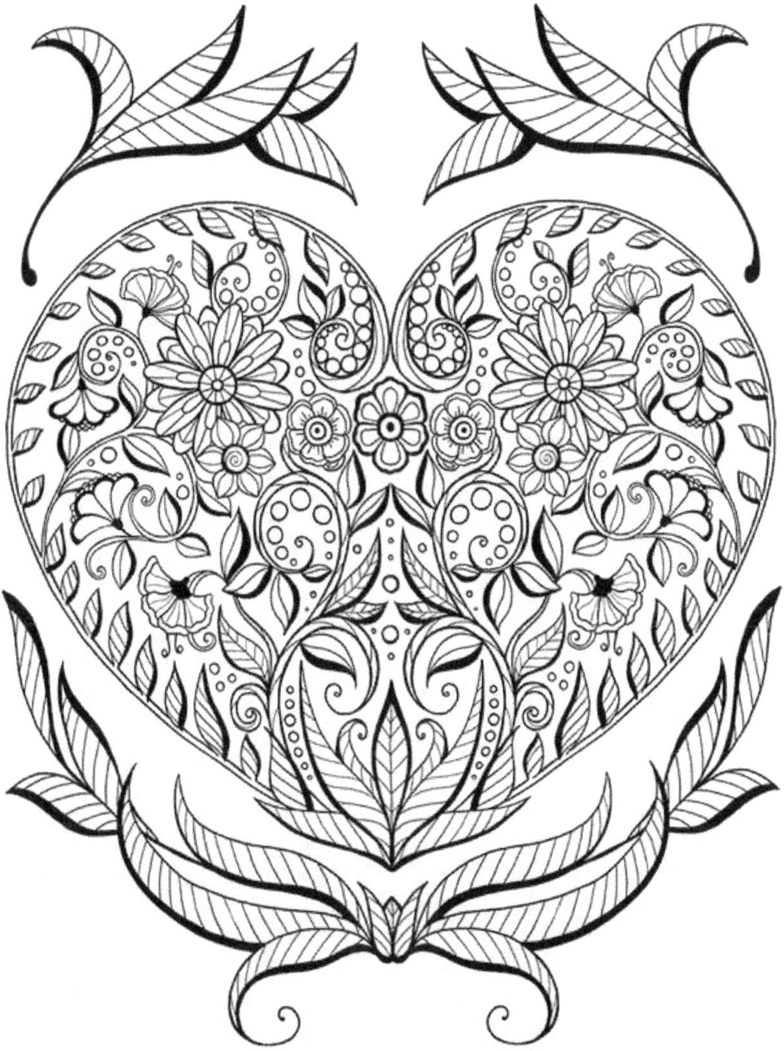

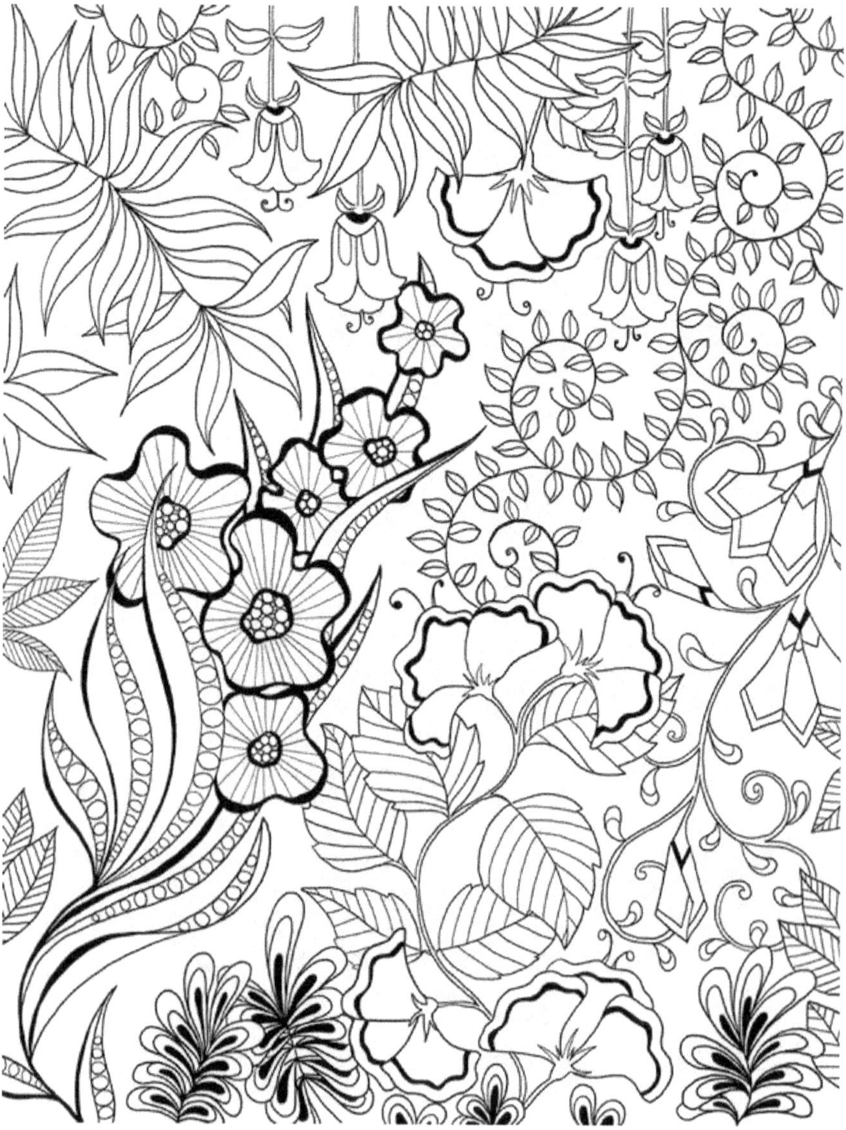

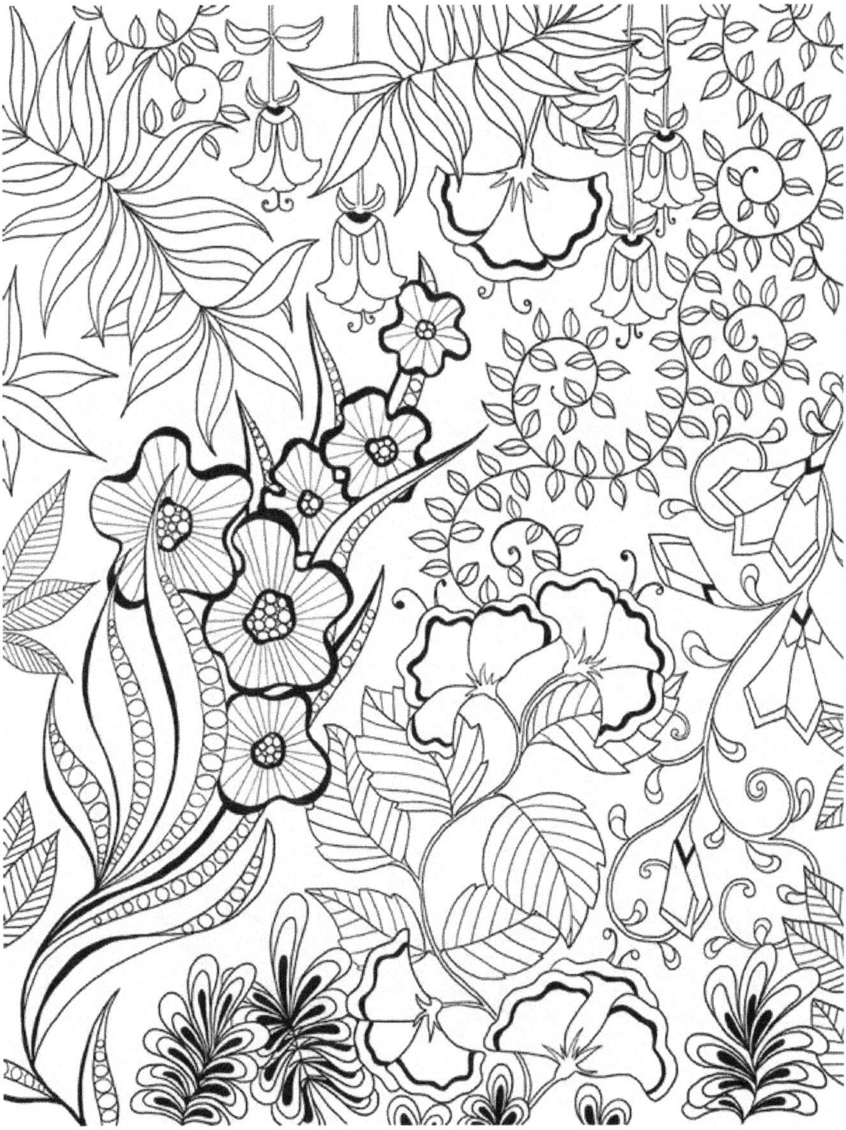

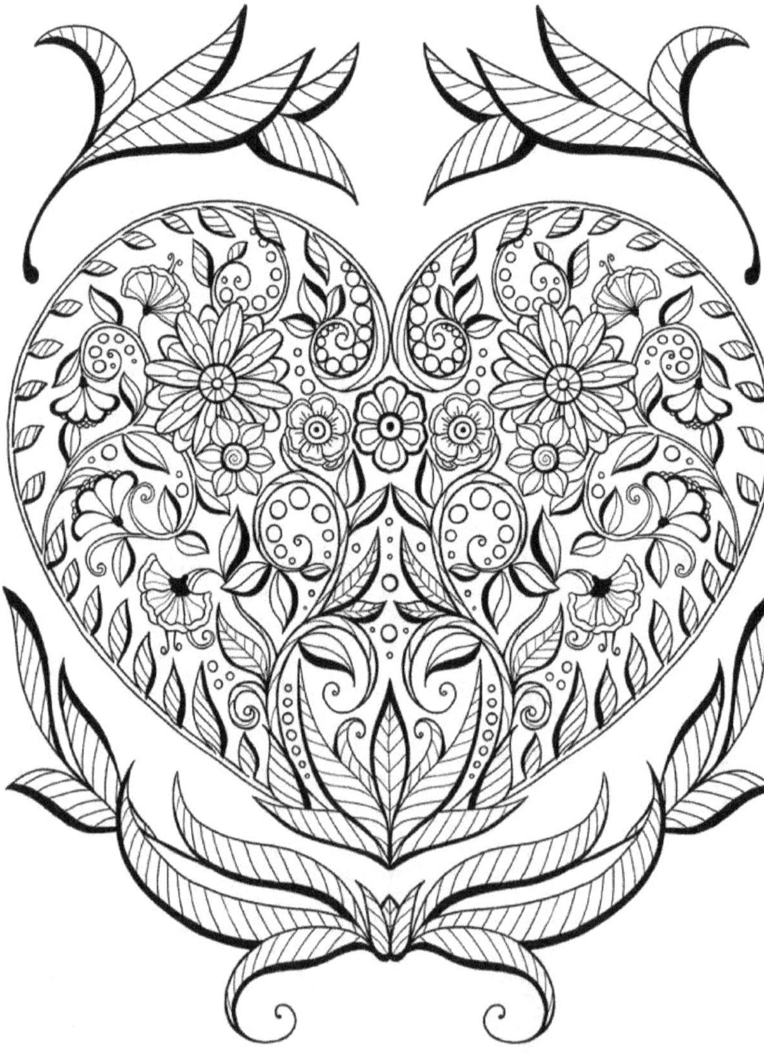

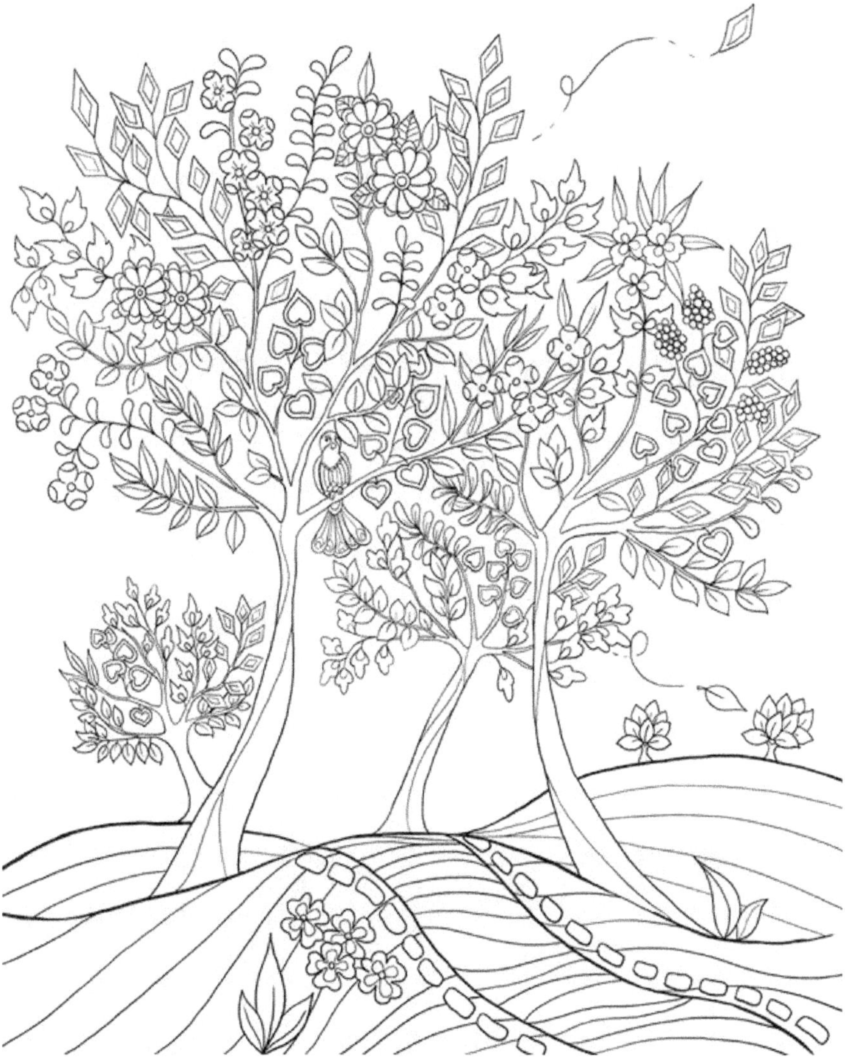

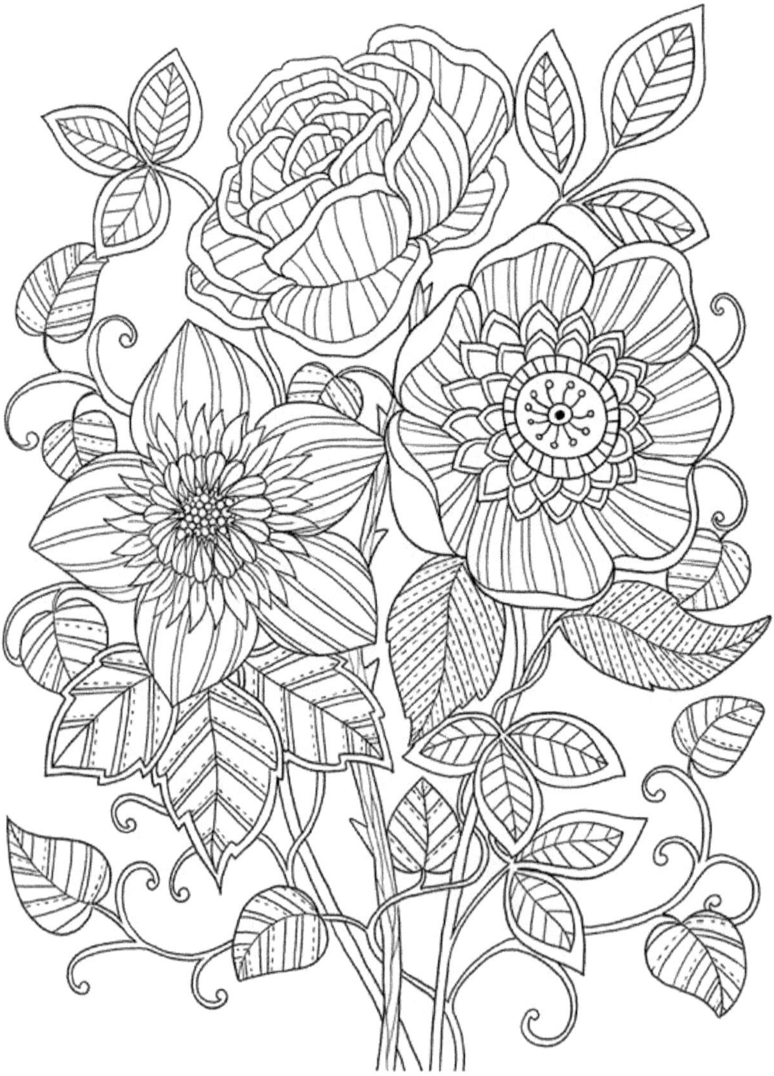

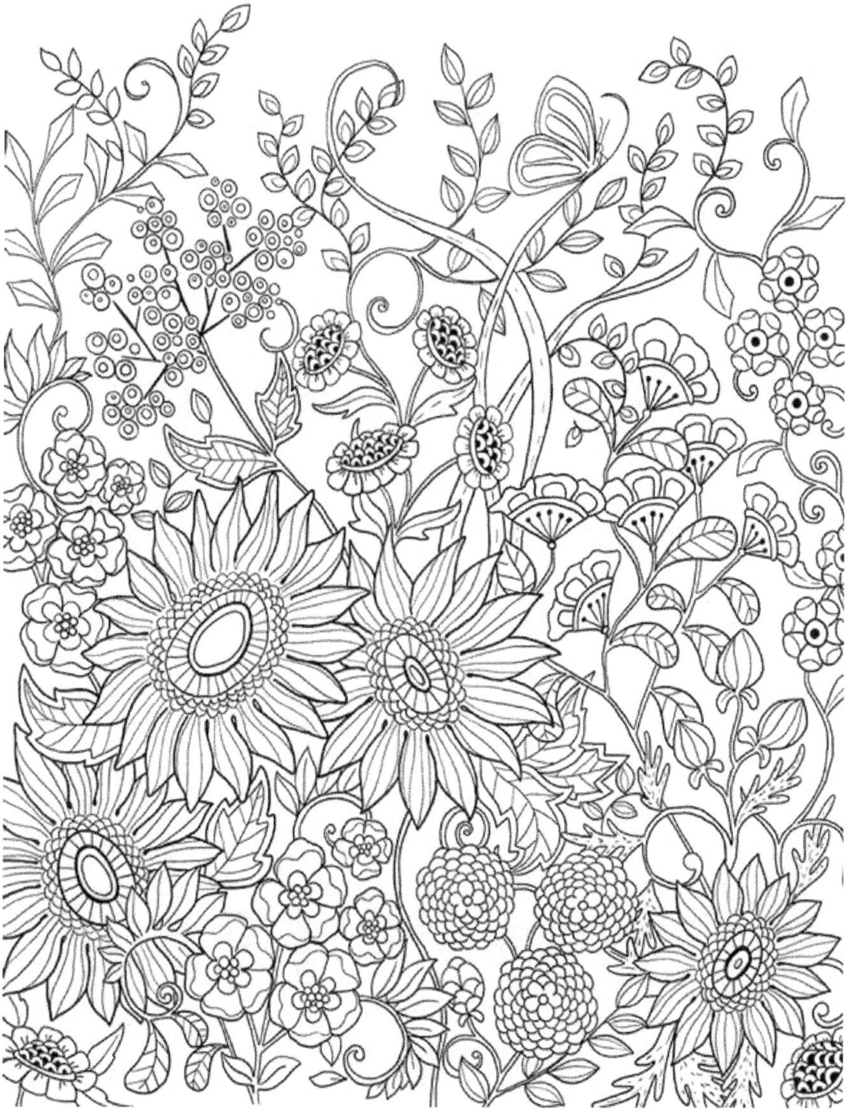

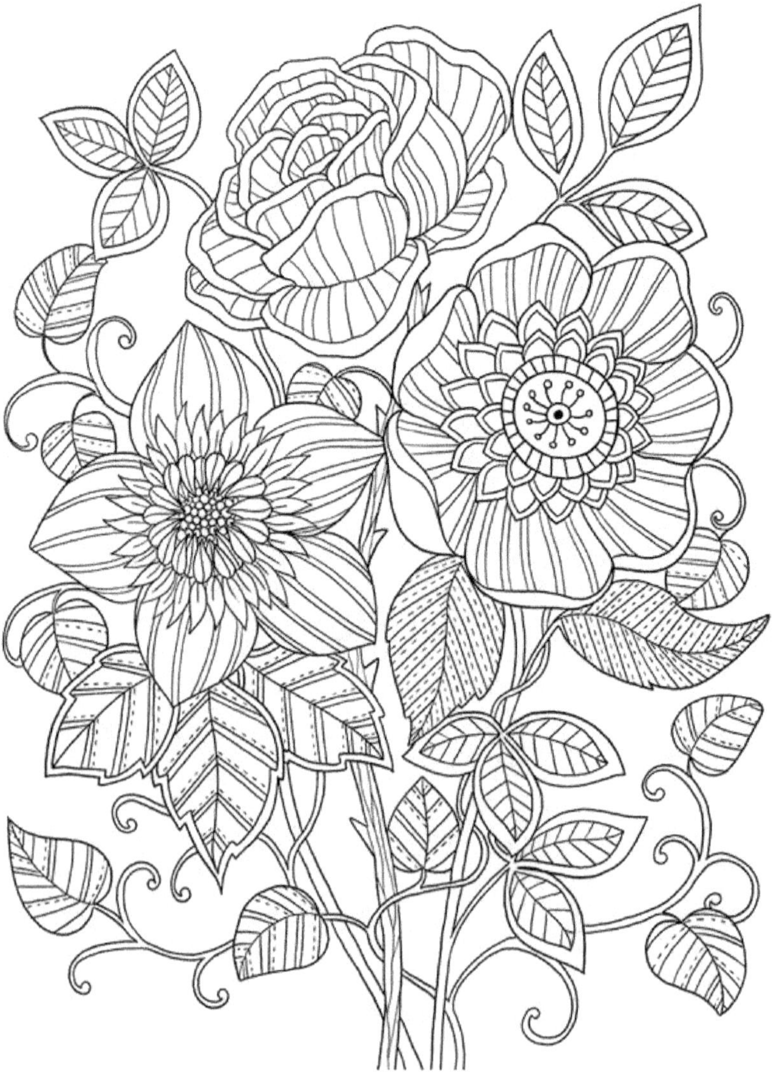

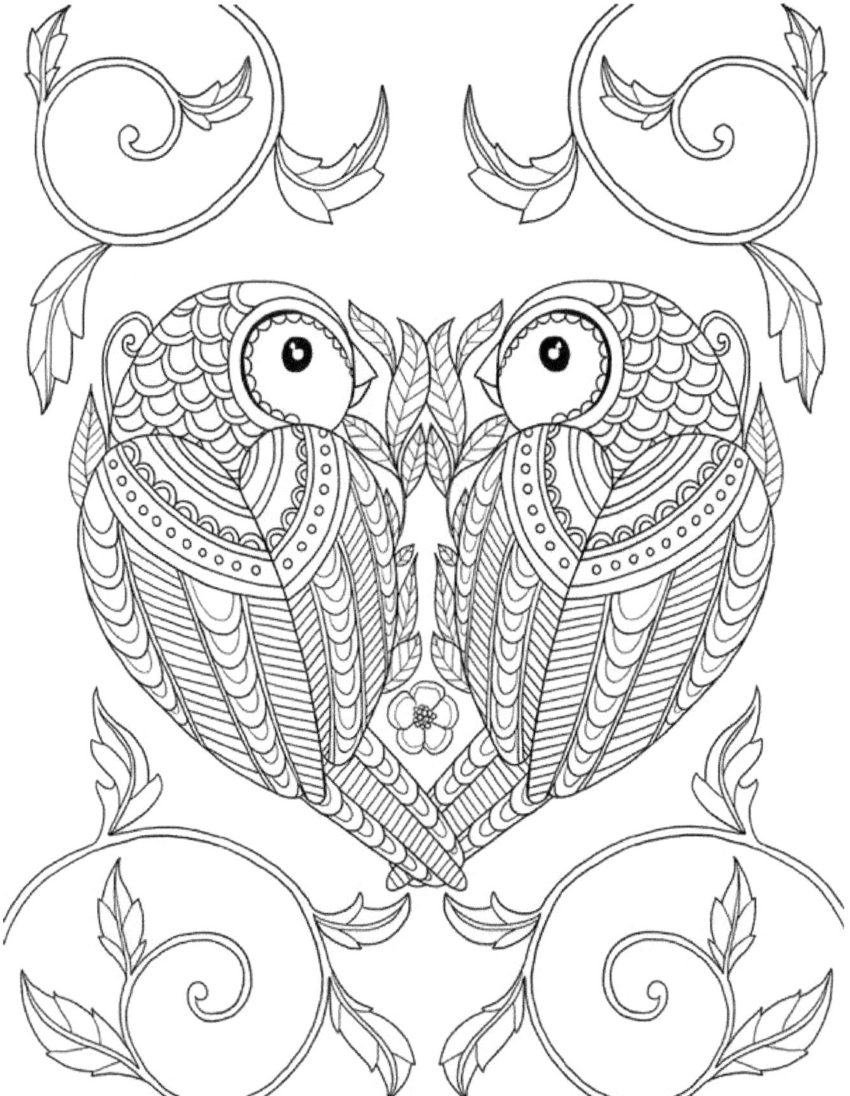

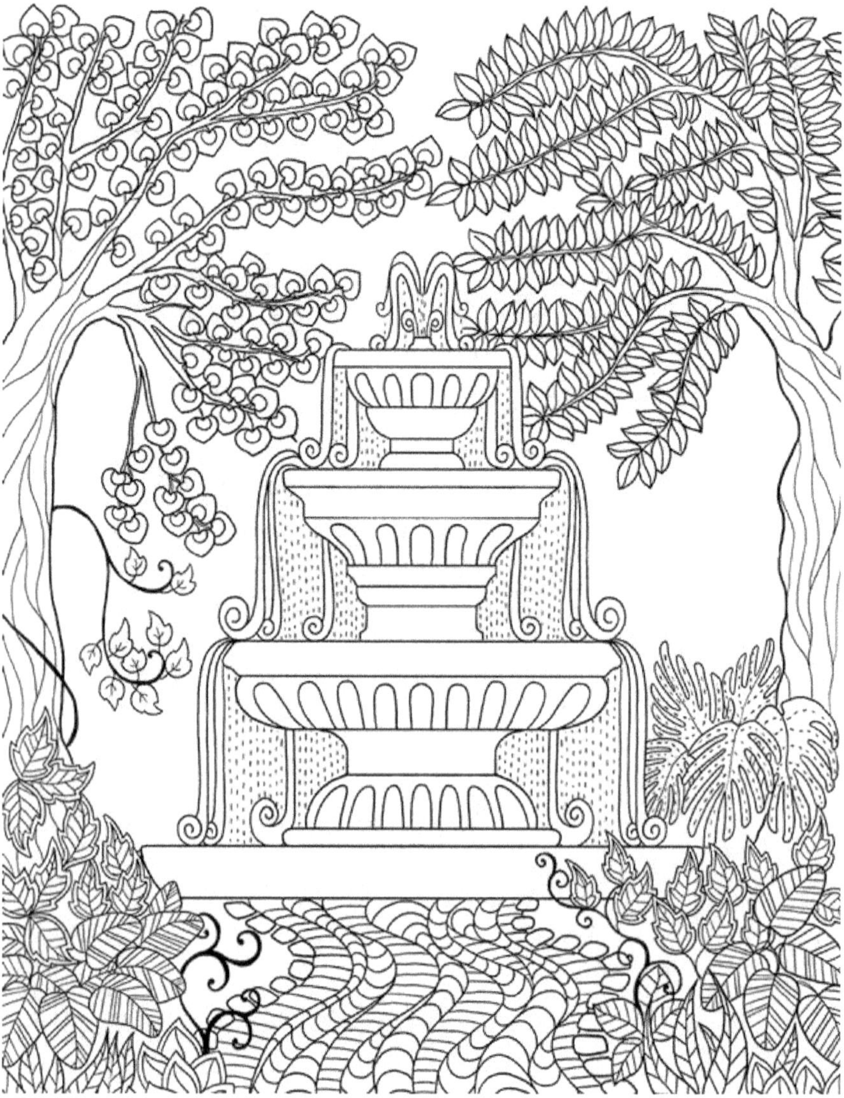

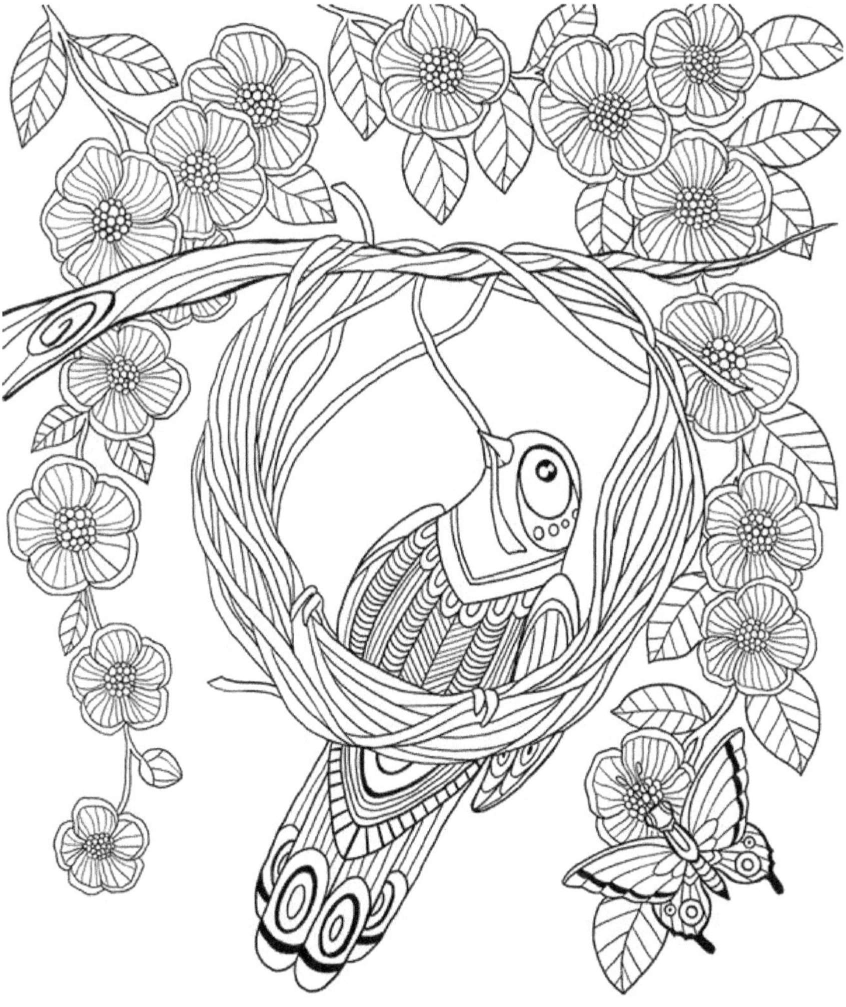

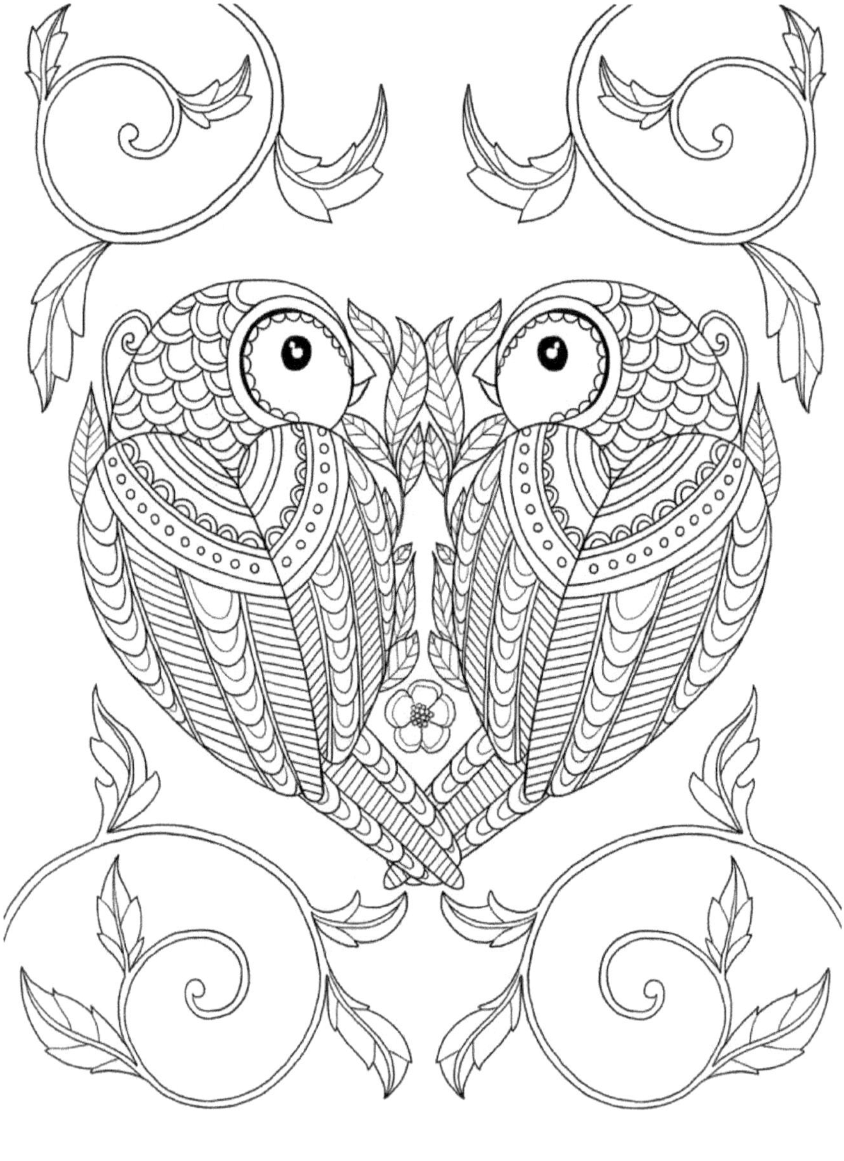

Other Recommended Books on Amazon: (Paperbacks)

Calm Your Mind Coloring Book

Relaxation Time Coloring Book

Mandala Coloring Book

Happy Coloring Books

Tibetan Mandala

www.ingramcontent.com/pod-product-compliance
Lightning Source LLC
Chambersburg PA
CBHW071000180526
45168CB00003B/1230
9781514397008